NAPOLEON HILL'S
KEYS TO PERSONAL ACHIEVEMENT

NAPOLEON HILL'S
KEYS TO PERSONAL ACHIEVEMENT

Napoleon Hill &
Judith Williamson

AN OFFICIAL PUBLICATION OF
THE NAPOLEON HILL FOUNDATION

SOUND WISDOM
P.O. Box 310
Shippensburg, PA 17257-0310

For more information on publishing and distribution rights, call 717-530-2122.
Reach us on the Internet: www.soundwisdom.com.

ISBN TP: 978-0-7684-1013-6
ISBN Ebook: 978-0-7684-1014-3

For Worldwide Distribution, Printed in the U.S.A.

Previous version published as *Conceive It! Believe It! Achieve It! Your Keys to Personal Achievement* ISBN: 978–1–937641–37–5

Written by Napoleon Hill

With contemporary commentary by Judith Williamson, Director, Napoleon Hill World Learning Center

Cover design by Eileen Rockwell

Disclaimer:
While efforts have been made to verify information contained in this publication, neither the author nor the publisher assumes any responsibility for errors, inaccuracies or omissions.

While this publication is chock-full of useful, practical information; it is not intended to be legal or accounting advice. All readers are advised to seek competent lawyers and accountants to follow laws and regulations that may apply to specific situations.

The reader of this publication assumes responsibility for the use of the information. The author and publisher assume no responsibility or liability whatsoever on the behalf of the reader of this publication.

Dedicated to all the readers of and contributors to the weekly "Napoleon Hill Yesterday and Today" articles.

FOREWORD

Dear Readers,

It's as simple as ABC but only in reverse!

Napoleon Hill states, "Whatever the mind can conceive and believe, the mind can achieve." This simple statement reminds us that the power of the Universe is within each and every one of us. By directing our mind in the path we wish it to go, we determine our ultimate destiny. Simple truths hold profound wisdom. But, just because the truths are simple, does not mean that they are easy.

To become accustomed to the process of using Dr. Hill's Science of Success System, we must condition our minds to be ready to accept the possible within the impossible. The two letters "i" and "m" in front of the word "possible" make many people retreat in fear and abandon their dreams. They allow these two little letters "i and m" to predict the future. If we just forget about that little threatening prefix "im," we can get on with the essential believing portion that precedes the achieving fact. The little autosuggestion, "If it's to be, it's up to me," helps dissolve the fear when the word "impossible" rears back and challenges us.

To believe in something prior to actual manifesting requires a person to have determined faith in overcoming the impossible.

Faith is a prerequisite to achievement. Applied faith is the very next, crucial step. When you apply your belief, you are then stepping into your future. A person with a purpose and a plan is undefeatable if this formula is leveraged well.

When our faith is in exquisite shape our end performance will be profound because we are removing all doubt about the picture perfect end result we have envisioned in the conceive portion of the formula. Faith is an elixir that performs exactly to our expectations. When the container of Faith is opened and the elixir is released, the essence is not easily coaxed back into the bottle. So, we must expect the very best when we unleash our faith in the outcome, and then apply steps to make our dream perform right up to our expectations. It's as easy as ABC but only in reverse!

Conceive It! Believe It! Achieve It!

It is my greatest hope that this little book of 52 essays from the archives will inspire you weekly to take appropriate action towards your dreams. Dreams come and go, but those that come true are the ones that you believe in without a doubt. When you believe in the power of your dreams you are compelled to take immediate action to make them a reality.

May all your dreams come true!

Be Your Very Best Always,
Judy Williamson

CHAPTER 1

Many times in life we make decisions that are not aligned with our purpose. These decisions have no staying power and soon are forgotten. Decisions that are aligned with your purpose embodied in your definite chief aim statement are remembered because they are truly significant to you.

—Ray Stendall

In considering linear time, it appears to exist in three parts: past time, current time, and future time. Past time might be defined as moving back mentally in time to consider what choices we made that contributed to where we find ourselves today—hindsight. Future time might be defined as moving forward mentally in time to consider what choices we can make today that can determine our future outcomes—foresight. Current time might be defined as the moment by moment time we exist in now and is the only "real" time we have. This present time best serves us when it is combined with insight, that quality that causes us to go inside ourselves for the purpose of considering what lessons are relevant for us to use in this our present moment.

We can watch a clock, turn the page on a calendar, journal our daily experiences, and chart the progress of time in numerous physical ways. Spiritually, our comprehension of time is different. It is more circular. We watch in our mind's eye a movie of our life and fast forward it to completion. All our experiences and connections are still inside of us and are very real. Sometimes these experiences become muddled together and the actual time sequence becomes blurred. We may see ourselves in dreams as children, and our own children may be our playmates. Or, we might recall an occurrence from our distant past and place people from our recent past in the scene. This is not dementia, but rather our mind attempting to made sense of our comprehensive experiences. Some scientists state that all time exists in the now. That is, there is no real distinction between past, present, and future time. Time just is. This might explain how events merge and blend together as one scene instead of a sequence of scenes in our dreamtime.

All this is interesting to consider, but in our waking world time marches on and we need to be in step with the marching band if we want to be in the parade! That is why Dr. Hill reminds us to use our time efficiently and wisely. Time is the essence of our being, and when we are out of time we cease to exist in this realm. So, if life is a checkerboard, the opponent against us, as Dr. Hill states, is *time*. Play the game to your best advantage by recognizing that time waits for no man or woman. Given this fact, you can then gain the insight that the best use of the time we are given is critical in our lifetime accomplishments. Be wise and use time to your very best advantage.

The Opportunity in TIME

Dr. Napoleon Hill

On the next occasion when you find yourself wasting a single second of this precious agent of OPPORTUNITY, TIME, copy the following resolution, commit it to memory, and start immediately to carry it out:

My Commitment to Doctor Time:

1. Time is my greatest asset, and I shall relate myself to it on a budget system which provides that every second not devoted to sleep shall be used for self-improvement.

2. In the future I shall regard the loss, through neglect, of any portion of my Time as a sin, for which I must atone by the better use in the future of an equivalent amount of it.

3. Recognizing that I shall reap that which I sow, I shall sow only the seeds of service which may benefit others as well as myself, and thereby throw myself in the way of the great Law of Compensation.

4. I shall so use my Time in the future that each day will bring me some measure of peace of mind, in the absence of which I shall recognize that the seed I have been sowing needs reexamination.

5. Knowing that my habits of thought become the patterns which attract all the circumstances affecting my life through the lapse of Time, I shall keep my mind so busy in connection with the circumstances I desire that no Time will be left to devote to fears and frustrations, and the things I do not desire.

6. Recognizing that, at best, my allotted Time on the earth plane is indefinite and limited, I shall endeavor in all

ways possible to use my portion of it so that those nearest me will benefit by my influence, and be inspired by my example to make the best possible use of their own Time.

7. Finally, when my allotment of Time shall have expired, I hope I may leave behind me a monument to my name—not a monument in stone, but in the hearts of my fellow men—a monument whose marking will testify that the world was made a little better because of my having passed this way.

8. I shall repeat this Commitment daily during the remainder of my allotment of Time, and back it with BELIEF that it will improve my character and inspire those whom I may influence, to likewise improve their lives.

You Can Work Your Own Miracles. Fawcett Columbine, 1971, pp. 118–119.

CHAPTER 2

One of the greatest strategies I have learned to deal with mental and physical pain is to think globally. What I mean by that is to think about the six billion people in the world and the various challenges people live with. They have gone through what you are experiencing and came out the other side and survived. That means you can get through it as well.

– Tom Cunningham

At times you may wonder how people withstand what they are going through in life. Seeing others experience suffering causes you to reflect on how blessed your life may really be. Many people are "in pain" emotionally, mentally, socially, spiritually, and/or physically and manage not to show it. In remembering this fact, the saying: "There but for the grace of God go I," is a good way to bring it all into perspective. At times, my plate is full of concerns and issues that I deal with in life, and at other times I am not as busy or preoccupied. When I have a moment to reflect on what someone else may be experiencing, I find that I become more compassionate as I relate to where they are coming from in life. Walking a mile in someone else's shoes truly does enable you to become more caring and understanding.

One of my goals this year is not to jump to conclusions or pre-judge anyone. If I feel like not talking to someone or not listening to someone's problems, I try to remind myself that I may be in similar circumstances myself in the future. Then, how would I feel if no one listened or even tried to understand what I was telling them? I would feel neglected and marginalized at best. At the worst, I would feel discounted or not worthy of their personal attention—in a word, dehumanized.

It is important to treat everyone with respect. If we model that behavior it will come back around to serve us. As you give respect you will receive it. Many perfectly capable people request special considerations because they feel that they have "earned" those privileges. In reality, they have not but are just asking for more because they can. Others who are truly in need soldier through and never request assistance. Entitlement is not an active word in their vocabulary.

I admire people who cause you to take a second look because of something they have not done. For example:

1. They do not request an exemption to the rules.
2. They do not look for pity.
3. They focus on others rather than themselves.
4. They give before they get.
5. They refrain from complaining.
6. They press on even when not feeling 100 percent.
7. They seldom talk about themselves, but rather ask you how you are doing.
8. They also inquire about persons significant to you.
9. They model positive behavior. And,
10. They acknowledge a Higher Power.

So, given the characteristics of those who walk the talk, isn't it time you ask yourself if you are on the pain-free program? Take the above ten-step prescription and check your results in a week!

The Benefit of Pain

Dr. Napoleon Hill

The greatest woman I have ever known, my stepmother, spent a large portion of her later life suffering almost unbearable pain from arthritis; yet she put into motion an undertaking which has already benefitted many millions of people and is destined to benefit yet untold millions, some of them as yet unborn. She was responsible for my early training which led eventually to my being commissioned by Andrew Carnegie to give the world its first practical philosophy of personal achievement.

Had my stepmother not been confined to a wheelchair, no one would have suspected she was in constant physical pain. Her voice was always pleasant and she conversed only in a positive trend of thought. She never complained, but always had a word of encouragement for all of us who lived close to her. I am sure that anyone who knew her, and understood the extent to which she had mastered physical pain, would have been utterly ashamed to have expressed fear of any form of dentistry or surgery. My stepmother's mental attitude toward physical pain was one of the major factors which made her a truly great person, loved by all who knew her, envied by some because of her profound self-discipline.

Thus we see, once again, that one's mental attitude toward physical pain is the determining factor which makes pain the master, or merely something to be transmuted into some form of beneficial service. Instead of thinking of her own physical pain and complaining about it, my stepmother directed her mind to helping others—particularly members of our family; and in that way minimized the effects of her suffering. This might prove a beneficial suggestion for all who allow their minds to dwell upon their own troubles.

You Can Work Your Own Miracles. Fawcett Columbine, 1971, pp. 58–59.

CHAPTER 3

Resolutions and the first of the year are also a time for reflection. And they often bring to mind other items of resolve and resolution over past years. You can't help it. The toughest answers, and the most important answers in your life, are the ones you have to give yourself. How you did it, or why you didn't get it done.

– Jeffrey Gitomer

Miracles take place every single day but they may slip right past our awareness if we have not tuned into their frequency. When we are scouting them out, our awareness is heightened and they appear right before us almost on command because we have correlated our desire with an intended outcome.

When you have your eyeglass prescription updated as I do yearly, the Doctor asks, "is it better now or was it better before?" as you peer into the machine. The forward and backward clicking of the lenses causes one to think about how we are forever changing in this sense of sight as well as in all other ways too. As we change our lenses so too does our vision change.

Life can be seen through rose colored glasses or through a glass darkly as the poet states, but we determine the lens we use.

20/20 vision is for many people a vision that is achieved only by wearing prescription lenses. The Doctor helps us achieve this goal through his or her training and capacity to correct or improve our eyesight. Likewise, our vision involving hindsight, foresight, and insight are visionary mechanisms that occur mentally and spiritually inside of us and can also be aided by another's prescription. Books we read and the people we meet to quote Charlie T. Jones, are the significant ingredients to an improved life. If we truly want to move forward and advance toward our destiny, we must work hard to reach that goal. As Jeffrey Gitomer, a student of Charlie T. Jones reminds us, we must work hard at our goal and not just expect the universe to deliver it gift wrapped on our doorstep. We must want it to happen, and then consistently work to make it so.

Miracles are hard work, but they do happen. They take more than wishing. They take physical effort, dedication, persistence, personal initiative, and preparedness before a like-minded universe graces us with the opportunity to see our open niche and to align with a miracle in the making. Our true best self, or what Napoleon Hill calls our higher self, is the key to recognizing this opportunity. Remember to set a goal, reach higher and higher, and then catch that miracle as it travels toward your best self. Much like a salmon swimming upstream, you can achieve your goal but it does not come without effort.

Thought

Dr. Napoleon Hill

We would emphasize that all thought, whether it is negative or positive, sound or unsound, tends to clothe itself in its physical equivalent, and it proceeds to do so by inspiring the individual with ideas, plans, and purposes for the attainment of desired ends, through natural and logical means. After thought on any subject becomes, through repetition a habit, it is taken over and automatically acted upon by the Subconscious.

It may not be true that "thoughts are things," but it is true that thoughts create things, and the things thus created are strikingly similar to the nature of the thoughts from which they are fashioned.

It is believed by many people, who are competent to judge accurately, that every thought which one releases starts an unending vibration with which the one who releases it will have to contend later; that man himself is but the physical reflection of thought put into motion by Infinite Intelligence. It is also the belief of many that the energy with which people think is but a projected portion of Infinite Intelligence which the individual appropriates from the universal source, through the equipment of the brain.

You Can Work Your Own Miracles. Fawcett Columbine, 1971, p. 133.

CHAPTER 4

I've actually found over the years that I can always do more than I think I can if I just get about doing it. It's the "getting about"—exercising the self-discipline muscle—that strengthens it. Or in the words of Jim Whittaker, the first American to summit Mount Everest, "You can never conquer a mountain. You can only conquer yourself."

– Karen Larsen

Daily we deny ourselves lessons that we can learn if we apply the standard technique of putting our nose to the grindstone. Accomplishments without work are few and far between—really, they are non-existent. Ask yourself when you have felt the sense of pride, the sense of achievement, and the satisfaction of a job well done? The only true answer is when you have done the task yourself. Watching someone doing the task, or hiring someone to do the task, does not have the same merit or satisfaction of doing the task on your own.

Remember when you learned to ride a two-wheeler? You progressed beyond being carried, pushed in a stroller, pulled in a wagon, and walking on your own two feet. Now, you were ready for the precarious ride you witnessed others in your age bracket accomplishing. Training wheels aside, the real sense of accomplishment came in when you sailed down the sidewalk without a parent's steadying hand and you were on your way! The freedom was exhilarating and the pride in your accomplishment was unmistakable. That's what conquering a milestone feels like.

Last summer my friend Dr. Judy Arcy and I climbed Apparition Hill and Cross Mountain in Croatia. With just a walking stick, tennis shoes, and our determination, we managed to accomplish both the hill and mountain on consecutive days during the late afternoon. Afterwards, we were both giddy because we did it! And, the joy of the accomplishment still brings us personal pride today. I hope that in the future we are both able to do it again too! It was simply amazing.

Life offers challenges that are ripe for the taking. Instead of standing back and saying "no" to the opportunity, be persistent and put one foot in front of the other. Slow but sure is a better forecast than never. Think you can, and you will—one steady step at a time.

Benefits of Self-Discipline

Dr. Napoleon Hill

Before you begin the study of the principles of self- discipline, we will outline some of the benefits which will accrue to you if you master this principle and put the ideas contained in this lesson into action:

- Your imagination will become more alert.

- Your enthusiasm will grow keener.

- You will develop greater initiative.

- Your self-reliance will increase.

- You will look at the world through different eyes.

- The scope of your vision will be widened.

- Your problems will melt away.

- Your personality will become more magnetic and you will find people seeking you who had previously ignored or overlooked you.

- Your hope and ambitions will be higher and stronger.

- Your faith will be more powerful.

No other single requirement for individual success is as important as self-discipline.

Self-discipline, or self-control, means taking possession of your own mind. This has been mentioned repeatedly throughout the course. You are now at the point where you can tie together the other principles which you have studied, and recognize the relationship which exists between them. All of the principles of this philosophy are for the express purpose of enabling you to develop control over yourself. The matter of self-discipline is one of the greatest of all essentials for success. Indeed, if one cannot master himself, he has little hope of mastering anything or anyone else.

PMA Science of Success Course, Educational Edition. Napoleon Hill Foundation, 1961, p. 267.

CHAPTER 5

Delivering more than required will raise your price tag,
and people will notice that. If they don't, you will, and you
will require more from life than what you are getting now.
It is a virtuous circle that will only begin with your action.

— Ken Kadow

Being a teacher by profession, I am always conscious of what potential result a lesson will have on the students. When a teacher instructs with the end in mind, he or she is focusing on the intended outcome for the class. By teaching with the end in mind, in a sense a teacher is like an alchemist who can change base metal into gold. The potential for gold is inside the students and already exists, however, it has not been refined and brought forward. A good teacher will create the opportunity for the student to refine himself or herself and change something ordinary into something extraordinary.

Many times as a student I was challenged by my teachers to live up to my potential. In each instance these special teachers indicated that they knew I could perform better than I was performing. My work was not always my best, but something mediocre intended simply to complete the assignment. When recognized as such, these teachers did me a favor because they alerted me as to my "higher self " or greater potential. If I exerted the effort, tried harder than was required for a passing grade, I could become something better than I was. By being put on notice, I knew that I no longer could settle for second best. I was not fooling them or myself. I had to achieve at the level of my capability, and when I did I felt a sense of pride that was equal to or even surpassed the additional effort.

These "scoldings" by a caring teacher enabled me to become the person that I am today. One professor who later hired me to work in his department told me in no uncertain terms to "reevaluate my commitment to his course," and another asked me what kind of student I thought I was by coming to class without paper and pencil for notetaking! The nerve of these people, I then thought. But without their admonitions, I would have merely survived and not thrived in my chosen field. Because someone noticed in me what I knew was a seed of untapped potential, I began to live up to their higher expectations as if these expectations were a given, or my true self. In time, I grew into the student they intended for me to become.

Wow! Teachers can and do wield a magic wand! Students who are susceptable to the magical spell will do well as they project themselves into their better future. Belief can create miracles. Hold up an expectation of higher performance for someone and watch the transformation take place. By knowing that you can succeed, you will. Someone just has to jumpstart that belief process! Try it out on someone you believe in today.

Personal Initiative

Dr. Napoleon Hill

Personal initiative means doing the thing that needs to be done without being told to do it. This is the self-starter principle. It starts the ball rolling. It gets action. It causes things to happen. Don't wait for things to happen; build a fire of personal initiative under them and make them happen.

There are people who have come all the way through life rendering extra service and yet have wound up in the poorhouse. They were absolutely honest, which gave everybody a chance to exploit them and they became draft horses for lazy persons who took advantage of their good nature and imposed upon them. There can be no compromise with honesty. A person must use wisdom and be careful about telling the whole truth to everyone. There are other persons around everywhere who can and will take advantage of the fellow who is naive enough to think that he can reveal all he knows about everything, because in doing so he leaves himself vulnerable to attack in vital spots.

And what about this habit of allowing people to impose on you, thus assuming the role of a draft horse? You must see to it that the law of compensation and the law of increasing returns work for you. It's one thing to cast your bread upon the water and wait for it to come back. But sometimes it comes back all moldy and soggy and unappetizing. The key to this strategic principle of going the extra mile is that you do it with purpose aforethought, or definiteness of purpose, counting on a fair return, sometime, somewhere. This is casting your bread upon the water and then keeping an eye on where it goes. Sometimes it is necessary to check on it and see that it starts on the way back, with maybe a little butter or jam on it.

PMA Science of Success Course, Educational Edition. Napoleon Hill Foundation, 1961, pp. 154–155.

CHAPTER 6

Numerous studies have found complaining to be detrimental to people's health, happiness, relationships and career. You would think that we would catch on to this and quit of our own accord. However, most people have no awareness of how much they complain.

— Will Bowen

There are days when we wake up, read the news reports, and decide that whatever we do is inconsequential and will not make a difference in the grand scheme of things. This negative attitude increases as we consider the world's capacity for problems over which we have no direct control. Whether it's politics, ecology, world hunger, education or catastrophic events, the "average" person feels left out of the solution process. We may not be part of the problem, but what really demoralizes a person and prevents one from taking action is not being a viable part of the solution either. What is a person to do when he or she feels shut out besides shut down?

If we decide to remain positive, it is always good to begin by reviewing what works versus what doesn't work. By focusing mentally on the positive potential and then taking immediate action for the change we envision, we can next begin the process for improvement. One baby step at a time may seem ridiculous but it was one step at a time that got us walking! If it worked for us, it may work for someone else. It is a proven fact that a single person, a small committed group, a room full of devotees to a cause, can and does impact outcomes all over the world. By taking a strong, positive stance and taking hold of an issue a person or a group can then begin to influence and soon change the outcome from negative to positive.

I have several Himalayan cats and in the winter when their coats change they are subject to matting. In grooming especially the older cats whose skin is thinner, this matting can be very troublesome. If I attempt to remove all the tangles in one grooming, I would not have very agreeable cats. But, I can work out a few of the tangles at a time and allow the cat to feel comfortable during the procedure. Rather than have them receive a "poodle cut," they retain their dignity and their beautiful coats by permitting me to address a single problem at a time. Life is like this too.

We can't do everything successfully at once, but we can do one thing at a time and make a huge difference. By focusing on that one thing that has importance for us, we can begin to change the world. It doesn't matter if we are saving the cats, the starfish, or the world, each effort has to begin with that first committed single step. Do it now for yourself and for the rest of the world. You can and do make a huge difference.

Control Your Destiny by Controlling Your Mental Attitude

Dr. Napoleon Hill

The person who controls his mental attitude may control his destiny.... Believe in the power of the spoken word and see to it that you speak no word which does not harmonize in every respect with your positive mental attitude. An essay by Dr. S. L. Katzoff will aid you in recognizing the importance of the spoken word.

The Spoken Word

- The greatest mischief maker is the human tongue.

- It is not what we say that counts, but how and when.

- Tactfulness will never dethrone the ego from its pedestal. Measure your words with the yardstick of courtesy, sentiment and gratitude.

- Conversational interest is based upon making another feel important, and replacing telling with asking.

- The less we say, the less we may have to take back. Nature knew her business when she gave us two ears and only one mouth. An unbridled tongue—even one word thoughtlessly spoken—may destroy the happiness of a lifetime.

- To prevent fault finding and bickering, invite criticism, give merited praise, quickly admit guilt, and do not hesitate to say "I'm sorry."

- Settle disputes as quickly as possible. Every moment of delay adds coals to the fires of dissension.

Finally, a reference table on successful conversation:

- Adopt a face to face method.

- Do not interrupt.

- Be responsible.

- Modulate the voice.

- Omit unfavorable references to the past.

- Give advice only when it is requested.

- Avoid negative comparisons.

- Applaud what you like and ignore what you don't.

- Never argue over unimportant details, for if you win, you will have gained no advantage.

- Guard your words and your words will guard you.

PMA Science of Success Course, Educational Edition. Napoleon Hill Foundation, 1961, pp. 231–232.

CHAPTER 7

You may begin to feel anger, resentment, disdain, confusion, or embarrassment when confronted by someone who does not agree with you or presents facts which contradict your beliefs. If you feel any of these emotions, there is a good chance that you may be blocking out the facts or opinions which if examined carefully could help keep you from making catastrophic decisions.

— Eliezer Alperstein

Accurate thinking is a learned skill. You are not born with it. In order to think accurately, you must make a firm attempt at self-discipline and self-mastery in order to cultivate the trait of objectivity. This is far easier said than done. The home, culture, neighborhood, religion, state, nation, continent, political system, etc., can and do limit our objectivity and therefore our ability to think accurately. It is like looking through a glass darkly as the saying goes. Sometimes we truly cannot see the forest for the trees! The trees are the learned biases, good or bad, and the forest is the neutral area that is beyond our learned differences. This is not always easy to discern.

Consider beliefs that you may "own." Where did these beliefs come from? Usually they are caught from our parents, role models, teachers, and others persons we have around us. But, these beliefs can cause us to have certain lenses on when we view the world. Through these lenses things either appear in focus or distorted, but the reality is that the thing we are looking at doesn't change, we do. For example, the world is a hotbed of current issues that focus on things people judge as being correct or incorrect, good or bad. For just the sake of a mental exercise, think of something that you do not believe in because it is against your system of beliefs. Now, take that topic and create an argument in support of that issue. Force yourself to see the opposite side and adopt the role of supporter when previously you were on the other side of the fence. Here you are attempting to create cognitive dissonance. Perhaps through this activity, you may adjust your viewpoint some and maybe even your system of beliefs. Likewise, you can do this same exercise concerning something you are sure is the right approach to an issue. Play the Devil's advocate to try on an opposing side.

When your opinions are rattled, your life begins to change. Life changes as we grow beyond our old system of beliefs. Thinking accurately aids us in this process. Decide to consider another's point of view, and whether in the end you agree or not, your worldview will expand.

University of Experience

Dr. Napoleon Hill

(In recalling a discussion, Napoleon Hill relates what was stated by Andrew Carnegie below.)

"There is no school which equals the good old 'University of Experience.' This is one school where 'cribbing' is not possible. One either graduates on merit, or does not graduate at all, and the teacher is the student himself. Skill is developed in every calling through the coordination of the faculties of the mind and the physical body. Such coordination is attained through controlled habits. But unless a man becomes action conscious, he will never become an organized thinker. He may think from morning until night, but he will never build a bridge, or manage an industry successfully, unless he acquires the habit of putting his theories to the test through action. Right here is where many men deceive themselves by believing they are organized thinkers. I have heard many men say, 'I have been thinking of doing this or that, but so far, I have found no way to do it.' The main weakness of such men is that they have left out of their thinking one important factor—physical action expressed through definiteness of purpose.

"If a man wishes to do something he should begin right where he is. Many will say, 'What shall I use for tools? Where will I get the necessary working capital? Who will help me?' Men who accomplish anything worthy of mention usually begin before everything they need is at hand. I have never yet been entirely ready for anything that I have undertaken, and I doubt if anyone else ever has been.

"Decisions have to be made, objectives chosen, and plans created for the attainment of the objectives. The man who hesitates to make a decision, when he has all of the necessary facts at hand, will never get anywhere. He will find himself outmoded by fast thinkers who express their thoughts in terms of action."

PMA Science of Success Course, Educational Edition. Napoleon Hill Foundation, 1961, p. 313.

CHAPTER 8

Over the years I have come to realize that so much more is going on in my life at a given time than I can ever know or experience. I have come to trust it is all ordered toward my ultimate good. I have pondered how best to stay mindful of being connected to this gracious care and offer some practices I have developed into habits that sustain me.

– Sr. Therese Sullivan

When I think of the purpose and plan the Creator has in each and every life, I am overwhelmed. Looking back it is often easier to see how we were gently guided to where we are today, but looking forward and understanding the absolute role Infinite Intelligence holds in our lifetime is much more difficult. Losses occur, dreams remain unfulfilled, people pass on, and we question the reason behind life itself. It does seem a bit bizarre that in the end all we worked for in our years on earth remains behind us as we transition. So, the obvious question is, "What is this life really about anyway?"

As an author of self-help books, lessons, columns, etc., it is easy to fall into the trap of advocating one type of action over another. Do this, not that! Do it now! Become self-actualizing. The commandments for success can go on and on and all a person need do is to follow them in lock-step movement, right? No, not really. We all recognize that there is a creative force bigger than even our imaginations can carry us that put us here. This Force created the entire Universe and us too, even if our own ego is too big to admit this fact. Therefore, it seems reasonable to assume that this Force may provide some sort of overt guidance and direction in our lives, even when we fail to acknowledge it or request it.

The ideas of chance, synchronicity, universal unconscious, subconscious mind, archetypes, and the collective unconscious are topics that attempt to get at the heart of what mankind truly is. But, as we all know, the jury is still out. There is no definitive answer for everyone to the age-old question, "What is Life?"

When I am confounded and troubled and wondering what next to do, I often recite the quotation, "Be still and know that I am God." This focuses me on the big picture and reminds me that in the grand scheme of things there is really someone out there who has my back. Each of us can rest assured that the Creator does care for the smallest details of everyone's life.

Cosmic Habitforce

Dr. Napoleon Hill

"The heavens declare the glory of God; and the firmament sheweth His handiwork" (Psalm 19, v.1) sang David, the inspired psalmist. And indeed the heavens are one of the most obvious and most awesome testimonies to the presence and power of this law of cosmic habitforce.

The stars and planets operate with clocklike precision. They never collide, never get off their appointed course, but roll on eternally, as the result of a preconceived plan. Infinite Intelligence is behind that plan. If anyone doubts the existence of Infinite Intelligence, that person need only study the stars and planets, and the precision with which they are related to one another, to become convinced of Its existence.

Another outstanding marvel of creation is the human mind, which is capable of projecting itself into the heavens and predicting astronomical occurrences to the moment, many years in advance of the actual event.

Back of this there must be order. Nature and the universe are organized and ordered. This order, or reliability, of nature simplifies life. It is not necessary to understand all of the laws and order of the universe to make them effective in our lives. They operate whether or not they are known or understood.

PMA Science of Success Course, Educational Edition. Napoleon Hill Foundation, 1961, pp. 489–490.

CHAPTER 9

So the next time you have an opportunity to read a book, remember good books can stir our imagination. Once your imagination is aroused, you can do as Napoleon Hill suggested when he said, "Whatever the mind can conceive and believe, it can achieve."

– Don Green

Have you ever considered the significance of reading? Slogans such as the three below can and do inspire the reader in each of us:

Today a Reader. Tomorrow a Leader.
Read, Lead, Succeed.
Expand Your Mind. Read a Book.

I can't imagine living a day without reading. It is second nature to me. I read to learn, to be entertained, to "armchair" travel, to crosscheck information, to learn "how to do it" for a million and one things, to enter someone else's mind and to improve my own life. Not much else in this world can promise all those outcomes for the cost of a book or an e-book.

When I read a good book that has enhanced my thinking, I recommend it to others in the hope that they may acquire the same enjoyment and knowledge. Books are varied in their scope and purpose. They can be "immortal" if they stand the test of time and live on in the printed word. Nothing else can carry words to us across the centuries and align us with the greatest mind from the past. For the writers of books, our thoughts and impressions can carry our words to a future we will not live to witness. Reading can be a time capsule or a rocketship. You just have to decide for yourself. Literally, the opposite ends of the spectrum serve to first give us a strong foundation, and second the capacity to dream. Roots and wings are the results of reading good books!

What have you read lately? Have you picked up a self-help book, a religious text, a good work of fiction, a children's story, a cookbook, or anything else that would fall within the category of something to read? The choices are endless.

A good reader finds enjoyment in reading. Books offer endless variety and serve multiple purposes in our lives, but unless you can "communicate" with the author by reading his or her book, you will never fully understand the dual approach of reading. Reading is not simply word calling or skimming for the juicy details, but a process that engages your brain and allows you to consider another's area of interest while you decode the message leading to the hidden treasure of thought!

My boss, Don Green, the executive director of the Napoleon Hill Foundation, is an avid reader as well. Even though our reading choices are not identical, we both find a good opportunity to swap the best books that we have read each month. This sharing serves us both well. Don has told me that he has no doubt that people with books in their homes are far better off than those without in many ways—financially, socially, mentally, etc. A home without books seems to be lacking in a prime resource for creating a charmed life. Why not pick up a book and read for thirty minutes a day? Do this for thirty straight days and then consider what you have gained. If reading in this way doesn't appeal to you, then read to a child. Any librarian will help you make good selections for their age group. In this manner, you will be sharing a skill that the young person can develop and use for a lifetime of riches.

How to Read a Book

Dr. Napoleon Hill & W. Clement Stone

There is an art to reading a self-help book. When you read, concentrate. Read as if the author were a close personal friend, and were writing to you—and you alone.

Now you recall that Abraham Lincoln, when he read, took time for reflection in order that he might relate and assimilate the principles into his own experience. It would be wise to follow his good example.

Also it is wise to know what you are looking for when you read a self-help book. If you know what you are looking for—you are more apt to find it. For if you really want to relate and assimilate into your own life the ideas that are contained between the covers of an inspirational book, work at it. A self-help book is not to be skimmed through the same way that you might read a detective novel. Mortimer J. Adler in *How to Read a Book* urges the reader to follow a definite pattern. Here's an ideal one:

Step A. Read for general content.

This is the first reading. It should be a fast reading, to grasp the sweeping flow of thought that the book contains. But take the time to underline the important words and phrases. Write notes in the margins and write down briefly the ideas that flash into your mind as you read. Now this obviously may only be done with a book that you own. But the notations and markings make your book more valuable to you.

Step B. Read for particular emphasis.

A second reading is for the purpose of assimilating specific details. You should pay particular attention to see that you understand and really grasp, any new ideas the book presents.

Step C. Read for the future.

This third reading is more of a memory feat than it is a reading task. Literally memorize passages that have particular meaning to you. Find ways they can relate to problems you are currently facing. Test new ideas; try them; discard the useless and imprint the useful indelibly on your habit patterns.

Step D. Read—later—to refresh your memory, and to rekindle your inspiration.

There is a famous story about the salesman who is standing up in front of a sales manager saying, "Gimme that old sales talk again, I'm getting kinda discouraged." All of us may become discouraged. We should re-read the best of our books at such times to rekindle the fires that got us going in the first place.

*Success Through a Positive Mental Attitude.*Prentice-Hall, Inc., 1960 pp. 239–240.

CHAPTER 10

I recall Dr. Hill's early years in Wise County. It was the love of his stepmother and her attitude towards life that completely changed his life for the better. How much can we change with a little PMA?

— Ana Laura Quesada

We never can be certain that our positive actions make a difference to others in this world. We can only hope that they do. As a teacher, I knew for certain that many of my students were there for a passing grade and not the lesson taught. Nevertheless, a few students resonated with the lesson and went on to accomplish their calling in life. What makes the difference? It's hard to tell.

Children from the best homes having all the perks oftentimes do far worse than their peers who have nothing extra or even anything at all to work with. No one can predict with accuracy the outcome for another individual— only educated guesses can be made. That's why they're called predictions and not a life sentence!

I always love the story of the starfish because it speaks to making a difference for people. If we work to make a positive difference in a person's life, I truly believe that we have given them a very special gift. We may not be able to do it for everyone, but we can make a difference for that special someone as the story of the starfish relates below. Ask yourself where are the starfish in your life? At home, at work, on the beach? For each of us, it may be different. But what is the same is the fact that if we take action we can make a difference for that one whose life we touched. It could be a simple smile, a warm "Hello," an extended telephone call, or any other intervention that we did not have to undertake. But, when our starfish find their correct home in the ocean, we will feel a sense of pride because we did make a profound difference for that one!

The Starfish Story

Originally told by Loren Eisley

One day a man was walking along the beach when he noticed a boy picking something up and gently throwing it into the ocean.

Approaching the boy, he asked, "What are you doing?"

The youth replied, "Throwing starfish back into the ocean. The surf is up and the tide is going out. If I don't throw them back, they'll die."

"Son," the man said, "don't you realize there are miles and miles of beach and hundreds of starfish? You can't make a difference!"

After listening politely, the boy bent down, picked up another starfish,and threw it back into the surf. Then, smiling at the man, he said, "I made a difference for that one."

Fondness for People

Dr. Napoleon Hill

Everyone who understands the nature of dogs knows that they instantly recognize whether people do or do not like them. And dogs express this recognition in no uncertain terms.

Most people are equally as discerning. They recognize, upon the slightest acquaintance, individuals who like other people. And they are attracted to the person who naturally likes people just as definitely as they resent those who have a dislike for people.

The law of retribution operates inexorably so that people are judged and dealt with not alone for their deeds, but for their dominating mental attitude through which they express their likes and dislikes with unerring definiteness.

It is inevitable, therefore, that people who dislike others will be disliked. And those who naturally like people will be liked. Through the principle of telepathy, every mind communicates with other minds within its range. The person who wishes to develop an attractive personality is under the constant necessity to control not only his words and deeds, but his thoughts as well.

PMA Science of Success Course, Educational Edition. Napoleon Hill Foundation, 1961, p. 183.

CHAPTER 11

Life to be sure has distractions and frustrations. When these events pop up, clarity of thinking can become fogged. It is important at this point, to take control of our thoughts and focus on what is really important and what it is we want from life. In other words, kick out the obstacles and negative thoughts that pop up in your mind.

– Dan Yovich

Controlled attention is the means by which we continuously work toward accomplishing our goals whether they are large or small. From the smallest task to the biggest mission in life, we achieve our desired outcomes by the art of focusing on exactly what we want, one action at a time.

Life can become overwhelming. Tasks at hand can seem insurmountable. People can become stymied, stagnant, and begin to stink in both the literal and metaphoric sense. Water that sits stagnates, animals that sleep too long without movement can become sick, people who relax on the job surprisingly find their co-workers making great strides. Next, many people who are left behind shake their heads and wonder what happened. Seldom do they see the connection between what they have failed to demand of themselves through controlled attention and the outcomes that they are now experiencing in the here and now.

When I become overwhelmed and need direction, I simply ask myself what is the very next simple action that I can take that will make a difference. I do what my mind suggests, and then I ask myself for the next action, and on and on. This may not be a profound formula for success, but it does work because it demonstrates that we are in control of our choices in life and can take control of the immediate time we have on hand. As we walk through this process, we will begin to notice that a small seed of enthusiasm is beginning to germinate within us, and as we return to the task again and again, the process becomes easier because we have emotionalized it. Whether you are doing dishes, sweeping a floor, sorting papers, or filing taxes, when you begin to see the end result in the not too distant future your attitude grows more positive and you begin to anticipate completing the work due to the sense of accomplishment that blooms within you. Sounds too easy, right? Well, it is.

Thomas Edison states, "When a man makes up his mind to solve any problem he may at first meet with opposition; but if he holds on and keeps on searching, he will be sure to find some sort of solution. The trouble with most people is that they quit before they start."

Limitations are self-imposed. Master yourself and next master the world.

Controlled Attention

Dr. Napoleon Hill

It is obvious, therefore, that when you voluntarily fix your attention upon a definite major purpose of a positive nature, and force your mind, through daily habits of thought, to dwell on that subject, you condition your subconscious mind to act on that purpose. As we have stated repeatedly, the subconscious mind acts first on the dominating thoughts placed before it daily, whether they are positive or negative, and proceeds to carry out those thoughts by translating them into their material equivalent. Controlled attention, when it is focused upon the object of your definite major purpose is the medium by which you make positive application of the principle of autosuggestion. There is no other means by which this can be accomplished.

The difference between controlled attention, and attention which is not controlled is very great. It amounts to the difference between feeding your mind on thought material which will produce that which you desire, or, by neglect, allowing your mind to feed upon thought material which will produce that which you do not desire.

The mind never remains inactive, not even during sleep. It works continuously by reactions to the influences which reach it. Therefore the object of controlled attention is to keep your mind busy with thought material which will be helpful in attaining the object of your desires.

PMA Science of Success Course, Educational Edition. Napoleon Hill Foundation, 1961, pp. 346–347.

CHAPTER 12

The perfect fit. It's not just a principle of sports, it's a principle of life. Finding our own perfect fit requires trying on a lot of different things and putting them to the test on the court. It takes courage, trial and error, and maybe even some crashing and burning, before our own Cinderella story is born.

— Elizabeth Barber

My remaining mentally alert and flexible a person creates a positive possibility for success to enter through life's side door. When least expected, opportunities show up and present new horizons in a person's life. Like a black swan these unexpected but welcome chance occurrences can alter the roadmap of a person's existence. Life gives us gifts that only can be opened when we are prepared and ready to receive them.

As I write this column, I am returning from the Third International Napoleon Hill Convention held in Kuala Lumpur, Malaysia. Our keynote speaker was Deepak Chopra and he did an outstanding job of lifting our consciousness to a higher level during his presentation. Founder and Chairman of Napoleon Hill Associates, Christina Chia, was the sole person responsible in organizing and promoting this event. As an agent for change and renewal, she is unsurpassed.

A group of us traveled together from Chicago via Hong Kong to Kuala Lumpur as speakers for the event. One individual, Tom "Too Tall" Cunningham, accompanied us with his wife Kim. Travel is hard for Tom due to his disability, but he made the commitment and shared his life's story with the participants at the Convention. His speech ended with a standing ovation and he was honored. Tom substituted praise for pain and stayed the course during his talk. This trip was an endurance test for him because of the constant movement, travel, and much walking required. But opportunity entered through the side door and the investment paid off! Preparing to board his flight home, Tom checked his iPad one more time and guess what he received? An invitation....

By being ready to accept what the Universe had in mind, Tom received an offer for a speaking engagement in Malaysia for this September. His eyes lit up and a huge smile covered his face as he sought me out to share the opportunity that came over his email. In his workshop, Deepak Chopra reiterated that chance is when preparedness meets opportunity, and this is exactly what happened with Tom. He has been preparing himself for nearly three years by always saying "yes" as he completed his leader certification course with the Foundation, "yes" when he returned as a newly certified instructor to be a mentor, and "yes" when asked to use his editorial skills in proofing materials free of charge. There were many more favors he granted to those seeking guidance or help, and sooner rather than later the Universe put him directly in the path of his dreams. He just had to continually show up and let the plan unfold!

By being ready to receive the Universe opens up an expressway to success. However, if your path to riches is being slowed by detours or construction, perhaps you need to embrace the unusual opportunities that appear in your life with a resounding *"yes!"* Don't hesitate, procrastinate, or rationalize as to why things will not work out. Just do it, and do it now! The reason behind the opportunity will become clear as the plan unfolds. Just ask Tom!

Flexibility of Mind

Dr. Napoleon Hill

Because a positive mental attitude will cause its possessor to have a charitable, interested and generous frame of mind toward those with whom he deals, it also follows that it will generate flexibility of mind. For if one is genuinely interested in another person and sees the good in that other person, he will be able to understand that person's ideas and attitudes and to have sympathy toward them even if such ideas and attitudes differ from his own.

Flexibility of mind is this ability to understand and sympathize with another's point of view or way of doing things, and to adapt one's self to harmonious operation with the viewpoints and ways of others. This does not mean that in order to achieve flexibility of mind one must be willing to change his own mind with every new thought, idea or custom which is presented to him. Indeed not! Such a person would be a spineless jelly fish and certainly would not be a pleasing personality. Flexibility of mind is simply the ability to understand, sympathize and harmonize with the ideas, attitudes and customs of others to such an extent that a pleasant, successful, working relationship can be established and enjoyed.

"Flexibility," said Andrew Carnegie, "was the one quality which gained for Charles M. Schwab the reputation of being one of America's greatest salesman. He could get down on the ground and play a game of marbles with a group of boys, making himself one of the lads for the moment; then get up, walk into his office and be ready to enter a master mind meeting where he was called upon to make decisions involving millions of dollars."

Life is one continuous series of experiences in salesmanship through which one must sell himself to every person he meets in his social, professional or occupational contacts. The person who lacks sufficient flexibility to enable him to harmonize his mental attitude with those of the persons with whom he comes into contact will not achieve a pleasing personality.

PMA Science of Success Course, Educational Edition. Napoleon Hill Foundation, 1961, pp. 166–167.

CHAPTER 13

Our personality is the one thing we can truly control and it can be our most accomplished strength or our greatest weakness. Irrespective of whom you meet, your personality should always be inviting, generous and constant. To limit the way you act or accept others based on skin color, religion, caste, race, or ethnicity reveals an internal disparity that can and should be corrected.

— Iqbal Atcha

The art of listening is a skill and a talent that can and does change the world. Everyone desires to be heard, but how many of us desire to listen to others? Are we always ready to invade a person's conversation with our own opinion, advice, and prejudices, or are we willing to listen and to learn from another's experiences in life? None of us know everything, and only through listening can we truly belong to the human race and share our common cosmic experience.

Napoleon Hill wrote on the subject of tolerance. To be tolerant of another, we must be willing to enter into their space and see life through their eyes. This magical role reversal is akin to the Vulcan mind meld that we all learned to imagine through Dr. Spock in the *Star Trek* series. Just imagine what the world would be like if we all consciously shared our experiences and thoughts simultaneously with others. Perhaps this technique is the one universal route to peace—the reciprocal process of sharing and receiving the gifts of another individual. Entering into someone's space and time allows us to receive the gift of a new perspective. This gift not only expands our world but has the capacity to change it too as ideas converge and create things anew. In many ways the Arts allow us to do this vicariously. As we sit in the theatre and listen to music or watch a performance we are in the moment and ready to receive the gift of the art form we are experiencing. Whether it is visual, auditory, or kinesthetic art, we experience the form and function of the piece and decide to assimilate it or not. This is another enduring capacity for growth and renewal.

Similarly, when connecting with people through active listening we decide whether or not we want to know more or move on. Regardless of our decision, we have shown our respect for someone's humanity by listening to them. This sharing grows into wisdom and wisdom can heal and unite the world. So lend an ear and learn a lesson. By listening more than speaking we can begin to acknowledge the divine spark in another and this spark can then kindle the light of wisdom that can indeed change the world.

Won't you stop and take the opportunity to hear another's story? It just might change your own.

Tolerance

Dr. Napoleon Hill

Tolerance is the disposition to be patient and fair toward those whose opinions, practices and beliefs differ from one's own. In other words, it is the maintenance of an open mind.

The tolerant person keeps his mind open to receive new and different facts and knowledge on all subjects. This does not mean that he will retain and adopt these new facts and knowledge as his own, but he will examine them and try to understand. Then he will endeavor patiently and wisely to reach a fair conclusion.

The intolerant person, on the other hand, has fixed opinions on almost everything. Moreover, he generally expresses his opinions freely and emphatically, and most often with the inference that anyone who disagrees with him is wrong. This is a trait of personality which never adds to one's popularity. The one thing which people resent most is open effrontery in connection with their own opinions.

Intolerance definitely limits an individual's privileges of appropriating and using the knowledge and experience of others. Instead of winning their cooperation, intolerance repels and makes enemies of those who would otherwise be friends. It stops the growth of the mind by cutting off the search for knowledge. It discourages the development of the faculty of imagination. It prohibits accuracy in thinking and reasoning.

PMA Science of Success Course, Educational Edition. Napoleon Hill Foundation, 1961, pp. 175–176.

CHAPTER 14

The first step toward acquiring wealth is to surround your-
self with helpful and supportive influences; to claim for
yourself an environment of culture, place yourself in it and
be molded by its influences and abundance.

– Gregg Swanson

How does a person cultivate hope? Is it as elusive as the butterfly and as invisible as a black cat on a moonless night?

The answer is both "yes" and "no." We attract hope when
we are hopeful and display a positive "you can do it" attitude.
By emitting positive energy, hope tiptoes up to us and before
too long we are nose to nose with this bubbling energy.

Recently I have been in Northern Ireland. The first day I
was outside watching a herd of cattle and reveling in the sheer
beauty of the landscape. I wanted to get a closer look at the
cows, and as I walked toward them they alerted each other and
quickly scurried to higher, safer ground. I felt abandoned and
annoyed as they eyed me from afar—a stranger encroaching in
their safe pasture.

On my last afternoon in the same location, I decided to
approach the cows once again. This time they took notice, and
I talked softly and stepped lightly as I approached the fence.

They did not move, so I advanced further. They recognized me. As if making a gesture of friendship, three cows from the herd started walking toward me. They were younger and probably foolish, but they were curious too. Before five minutes passed more came and soon I had a single file lineup of thirteen cows along the fence line. New ones continued to join the others as they felt safe in my presence. This was one of those timeless moments for me. I recalled the final scene from the movie *City Slickers,* and felt the tangible goodness of nature all around me.

Both I and the cows were hopeful that neither of us meant to harm the other. By suspending our inhibitions, a moment of peaceful unity was enjoyed. It felt good to experience a letting go of fear and a moment of community. Hope can be renewed, and hope can foster peaceful relationships. Take the first step and you can never tell who will join you on the path to riches.

You can be instrumental in creating these positive effects yourself, but first you have to take that initial step. Let's practice.

Motivate Yourself and Others

Dr. Napoleon Hill & W. Clement Stone

Motivate yourself and others with the magic ingredient.

What is the magic ingredient?

One man, in particular, found it. Here is his story.

Some years ago, this man, a successful cosmetic manufacturer, retired at the age of sixty-five.

Each year thereafter his friends gave him a birthday party, and on each occasion they asked him to disclose his formula. Year after year he pleasantly refused; however, on his seventy-fifth birthday his friends, half jokingly and half seriously, once again asked if he would disclose the secret. "You have been so wonderful to me over the years that

I now will tell you," he said. "You see, in addition to the formulas used by other cosmeticians, I added the magic ingredient."

"What is the magic ingredient?" he was asked.

"I never promised a woman that my cosmetics would make her beautiful, but I always gave her hope."

Hope is the magic ingredient!

Hope is a desire with the expectation of obtaining what is desired and belief that it is obtainable. A person consciously reacts to that which to him is desirable, believable, and attainable.

And he also subconsciously reacts to the inner urge that induces action when environmental suggestion, self-suggestion, or auto-suggestion cause the release of the powers of his subconscious mind. His response to suggestion may develop obedience that is direct, neutral, or in reverse action to a specific symbol. In other words, there may be various types and degrees of motivating factors.

Every result has a given cause. Your every act is the result of a given cause—your motives.

Success Through a Positive Mental Attitude. Prentice-Hall, 1960, pp. 102–103.

CHAPTER 15

I drifted in spite of being Napoleon Hill's grandson. And I drifted inspite of being able to bear witness to the truth of his words. I drifted for 25 years because I possessed job security. I was reasonably well paid. I felt good about myself. I drifted because I had no reason to change. But most of all, I drifted because I had no long term goals, no burning desire.

— J. B. Hill

The process of change is keyed to our evolution. Without change and renewal, no growth can occur. To change, we must become aware of our need for it. Shakespeare writes about the seven ages of man and as a person reflects on these stages of human development, we know that the process happens, but for some of us it doesn't go smoothly. Too often a person may become stuck in a stage and resist change. When that happens, time marches on and the person doesn't. Recognizing that change is aligned with growth, a person can develop a positive outlook toward change and instead of fearing it a person can learn to embrace it.

Émile Coué remarked in his famous affirmation that, "Every day in every way I get better and better." This thought coupled with Dr. Hill's statement, "What the mind can conceive and believe, it can achieve," can be two powerful tools that are instrumental in disciplining and motivating ourselves. Thoughts are powerful things, but only useful when they are put into action. To become better day by day, you must first consider what you want to improve about yourself. But that in itself is not enough. Next, you must discipline yourself to take action by doing the very thing you have been thinking about doing.

Thought + Action = Success

Add emotion to the action, and the new and improved formula becomes even more powerful—just like Dr. Hill's mental dynamite!

Thought + Emotional Action = Success!

Try it and see.

Think of change as growth. Ask yourself how you desire to improve and grow. Target a specific area in your life and then think about it. Work your thought up to an emotionalized white, intense heat of desire and then see if your actions parallel this intensity of emotion. If they do, you are on the high road to personal improvement, if not; you can only hold yourself accountable. You are the you who holds the key to your success. Nothing holds you back except yourself. Get out of your own way, and move forward. You can do it if you believe you can!

Do You Drift Aimlessly Through Life?

Dr. Napoleon Hill & W. Clement Stone

Think of it! Think of the people who drift aimlessly through life, dissatisfied, struggling against a great many things, but without a clear-cut goal. Can you state, right now, what it is that you want out of life? Fixing your goals may not be easy. It may even involve some painful self- examination. But it will be worth whatever effort it costs, because as soon as you can name your goal, you can expect to enjoy many advantages. These advantages come almost automatically.

1. The first great advantage is that your subconscious mind begins to work under a universal law: "What the mind can conceive and believe, the mind can achieve." Because you visualize your intended destination, your subconscious mind is affected by this self-suggestion. It goes to work to help you get there.

2. Because you know what you want, there is a tendency for you to try to get on the right track and head in the right direction. You get into action.

3. Work now becomes fun. You are motivated to pay the price. You budget your time and money. You study, think, and plan. The more you think about your goals, the more enthusiastic you become. And with enthusiasm your desire turns into a burning desire.

4. You become alerted to opportunities that will help you achieve your objectives as they present themselves in your everyday experiences. Because you know what you want, you are more likely to recognize these opportunities.

Success Through a Positive Mental Attitude. Prentice-Hall, 1960, p. 25.

CHAPTER 16

The brain is very good at "caution." In fact, the brain is much more likely to avoid risk than it is to seek associated rewards. "Fear" is the method by which the brain protects us. Unfortunately, it also works against those of us striving for success. It is impossible to achieve success without some risk, some fear. If nothing else, we fear the embarrassment of failure. Achieving success means that we must conquer our fear.

– J. B. Hill

The good news is that our mental programming can be changed because we are soft-wired rather than hard-wired. This fact holds great hope for every wife, husband, mother, father, child, or friend on the planet who wishes someone would change for their own good. Change for good is possible, however, the only person who can initiate and accomplish that change is *you!* Ironically, when you change, the world changes right along with you. Remember this fact.

In grade school, I recall the Nuns telling us not to single someone out by pointing at them. They reminded us that when we point with our index finger in an accusatory manner most of our fingers are pointing right back at us. This is a good fact to recall because when we feel someone needs to change, the reality may very well be that it is us that needs the makeover. Scapegoats aside, when we look in the mirror, it is our image we see. This should be our first clue that change needs to begin with us.

Each of us lives within ourselves and battles with our ego daily. Lack of discipline, lack of self-control, poor work ethic, moral weaknesses, etc., all can be blamed on someone or something else, but the final realization is that each of these traits can only be traced back to the source—our personal character—good or bad.

Time allows us to make changes that we deem necessary. Our growth is contingent upon our awareness. As we learn, we grow in wisdom and years. Isn't it a comforting thought to realize that we can overcome past mistakes, improve our personal success profile, and reach our potential by adjusting our habits? I for one am glad that I have been given multiple chances to get it right. It may take me multiple times to perfect something, but then in the end what I have attained I am proud of because of the effort that I exerted in bringing an improved version of myself forth.

Ruled by Habits

Dr. Napoleon Hill

Cosmic habitforce controls all human relationships and determines whether an individual will be a success or a failure in his life work. For nature uses this law as a medium by which every living thing is forced to take on and become a part of the environment in which it lives and moves daily. All of us are ruled by habits. They are accepted by us because of repeated thoughts and experiences. Therefore, we can control our earthly destiny to the extent that we control our thoughts. As we have seen, our thought habits, our mental attitude, are the one and only thing over which each individual has the right of complete control.

You create patterns of thought by repeating certain ideas, or behavior, and the law of cosmic habitforce takes over those patterns and makes them more or less permanent (depending upon the intensity with which they are repeated or practiced) unless or until you consciously rearrange them.

Man is the only living creature equipped with the power of choice through which he may establish his own thought and behavior patterns, or habits, or break them and rearrange them at will.

But while the Creator has given man the privilege of controlling his thought, He has also subjected man to the law of cosmic habitforce through which his thought habits must invariably clothe themselves in their physical likeness and equivalent. Cosmic habitforce does not dictate what thoughts a man must express, but it takes over whatever he does think and do, and sees to it that man's thoughts and actions go on to fulfill the measure of their creation.

If a man's dominating thoughts are of poverty, the law translates these thoughts into physical terms of misery and want. But if a man's dominating thoughts are of happiness and contentment, peace of mind and material wealth, the law transforms them into their physical counterpart. Man builds the pattern through his dominating thoughts, while the law of cosmic habitforce casts the mold according to the patterns man develops.

PMA Science of Success Course, Educational Edition. Napoleon Hill Foundation, 1961, p. 491.

CHAPTER 17

Going the Extra Mile is Personal Initiative in action, for without the motivation to succeed, it is hard enough to go the first mile, let alone the extra one. Since the idea of Going the Extra Mile is usually confusing and sometimes even offensive to those who hear it for the first time, this suggests that self-motivation is less common than we would like to think.

— Christopher Lake

Are you a starter or a finisher? Ideally, you should be both, but most people fall into the "starter" category and end up staying there. Unlike in sports, this is not a good position to play in life because by being a starter and not a finisher you never reach your potential for greatness. Starters have enthusiasm, but lack persistence. They dream about the outcome, but never devise an organized plan to achieve the end in mind. They stumble and fall and never get up. They don't push onward or upward because the struggle appears too great. If any of these descriptions apply to you, then surely you are destined to stay on the failure side of the river of life that Dr. Hill describes. Only through personal initiative backed by fearless persistence will you cross over to the success side of the river.

Many people sign up for our courses and indicate that they want to complete the three step curriculum towards Leader Certification, but few finish the process. What happens to most is that life intervenes and they drop out when it is easier to quit than to persist. Money, time, personal hardships, etc., are all offered as "legitimate" excuses for incompletion, but in reality the lack of personal initiative is the root cause. Life happens to every single one of us, but those who succeed have the conviction of their dreams plus the fortitude to work towards them. Glory requires guts.

Dr. Hill states: "The mind that has been made to receive, attracts that which it needs, just as a magnet attracts steel filings." In order to receive you must be open to making a start, and once that channel is open because you have made a start your mind will attract the means and methods needed to complete whatever task you set before yourself. The key to unlocking the door to success is personal initiative followed by sustained action coupled with persistence. Without a motive and a customized plan to achieve it, you will remain a "starter" in life. Begin today with a desire to complete something, anything, that you want to achieve and right here and now write out a step-by-step plan to accomplish it. This is the most important part of the process, because once the directions are defined for your journey, all you have to do is begin the trip one step at a time. And, in no time you will be a "finisher" and have crossed over to the success side of the river of life and not swept away with the current distractions that life places in everyone's path.

Personal Initiative

Dr. Napoleon Hill

"The man who gets ahead," Carnegie continued, "does the thing that should be done without being told to do it. But he doesn't stop there; he goes the extra mile by doing a great deal more than is expected or demanded of him."

Personal Initiative bears the same relationship to an individual that a self-starter bears to an automobile! It is the power that starts all action. It is the power that assures completion of anything one begins.

There are many "starters" but few "finishers." Personal Initiative is the dynamo that pushes the faculty of the imagination into action. It is the process of translating your definite major purpose into its physical or financial equivalent. It is the quality that creates a major purpose, as well as all minor purposes.

PMA Science of Success Course, Educational Edition. Napoleon Hill Foundation, 1961, p. 201.

CHAPTER 18

Rural areas like Hill's birthplace of Wise County, Virginia, have historically been judged by their poorest people; nevertheless, there are those who prove that success can bloom anywhere, particularly in the mountains of Appalachia, where the values of many align with Napoleon Hill's principles.

– Amy Clark

Perhaps you have heard of the actor Bruce Lee. In 1969, he wrote, "*My Definite Chief Aim.* I, Bruce Lee, will be the first highest paid Oriental super star in the United States. In return I will give the most exciting performances and render the best of quality in the capacity of an actor. Starting 1970 I will achieve world fame and from then onward till the end of 1980 I will have in my possession $10,000,000. I will live the way I please and achieve inner harmony and happiness."

Sounds familiar doesn't it? Perhaps you have read the steps to this formula somewhere before—I know that I have! Considering that Bruce Lee was well on his way to achieving his DCA prior to his death, I now ask you:

Have your written down your Definite Chief Aim in life?
If not, why not?

It's simple. In Dr. Hill's own words below I have included the six steps contained in the formula. Why not take an hour out of your day right now and assemble your life's mission? This is important because it contractually sets the pace from today onward of who you are becoming. It is as important as a legal contract so why not date it and sign it?

Heck—even have it notarized and witnessed by a trusted associate. In your very best handwriting, author your life's Definite Chief Aim following Dr. Hill's six steps to riches. Date it. Sign it. Reread it out loud twice daily—morning and evening. Work your desire up into a white-hot intensity of desire, or as Dr. Hill calls it—a burning desire. Mentally see, hear, taste, smell and touch your outcome in your mind's eye. Make it as real to the senses as you possibly can. Immediately, take action—whatever action—to pull your dream into this reality of time and space. You can do it because you believe you can.

Six Ways to Turn Desires Into Gold

Dr. Napoleon Hill

The method by which desire for riches can be transmuted into its financial equivalent, consists of six definite, practical steps, viz:

First: fix in your mind the exact amount of money you desire. It is not sufficient merely to say "I want plenty of money." Be definite as to the amount. (There is a psychological reason for definiteness which will be described in a subsequent chapter.)

Second: determine exactly what you intend to give in return for the money you desire (There is no such reality as "something for nothing.")

Third: establish a definite date when you intend to possess the money you desire.

Fourth: create a definite plan for carrying out your desire, and begin at once, whether you are ready or not, to put this plan into action.

Fifth: write out a clear, concise statement of the amount of money you intend to acquire, name the time limit for its acquisition, state what you intend to give in return for the money, and describe clearly the plan through which you intend to accumulate it.

Sixth: read your written statement aloud, twice daily, once just before retiring at night, and once after arising in the morning. As you read—see and feel and believe yourself already in possession of the money.

It is important that you follow the instructions described in these six steps. It is especially important that you observe, and follow the instructions in the sixth paragraph. You may complain that it is impossible for you to "see yourself in possession of money" before you actually have it. Here is where a burning desire will come to your aid. If you truly desire money so keenly that your desire is an obsession, you will have no difficulty in convincing yourself that you will acquire it. The object is to want money, and to become so determined to have it that you convince yourself you will have it.

Think and Grow Rich. Fawcett Books, 1963, pp. 36–37.

CHAPTER 19

The class talked about how they could apply different principles in different aspects of their current life. An example given was working for a negative boss. We talked about going the extra mile and maintaining a positive mental attitude in this type of situation and not stooping down to the negative boss' level. It was fun and exciting watching the students grow, because this was their first introduction to Napoleon Hill.

— Michael Collins

It is always uplifting to receive positive commentary from people I have worked with in my position as Director of Education for the Napoleon Hill Foundation. Today I received a report from Michael Collins regarding a class that he is teaching as a final project for his Leader Certification.

Once or twice yearly, the Napoleon Hill World Learning Center conducts International Leader Certifications for those individuals who have a burning desire to share their love of Napoleon Hill's Philosophy of Success as part of their life's mission. In advance, they complete two courses in order to prepare for this certification class—one being a home study course, and the second being an internet course. Once completed successfully, these students then may advance to qualify for the final course—Leader Certification.

Each student enters the course because they have *already* decided the use that they want to put the material to in their life. Here is a response that I wrote to a person wanting to know what could be done with the certificate once earned:

> Do not be mistaken. This is a self-help motivational series of courses designed to assist you in working primarily with yourself and then with others as a leader with a certificate of completion from the Foundation. It is not a license or a partnership for employment through the Foundation. This is not a franchise agreement, although we do those for yearly fees for international countries. As with any diploma from a school of study, such as a BA in English or BS in Science, the school from which you graduate does not employ you or find you a job. We can point you in a direction such as local community colleges (if you have the prerequisites to teach), prisons (if prisons in your area are open to this type of instruction), religious centers, etc., but ultimately what you do with your new found learning and knowledge depends upon your own personal persuasion and initiative. Please watch the video that Ray Stendall did on our website at www.naphill.org and read again the page on our website about what you can do with our leader certification once you complete the process.

I just do not want any misunderstanding to occur. Since you asked the question, I am responding to it as truthfully as I know how. The majority of people use this training within their area of employment—they instruct their staff or offer courses for distributors or agents. Many of our instructors are in the field of insurance, sales, teaching, religious studies, real estate, etc., and apply this knowledge to their immediate area of interest within their current area of employment. I hope this helps you make an informed decision about our courses.

Thank you for the inquiry.

As you can read, I advocate full disclosure. With that being said, if you decide to measure up, take control of your life, and use personal education for the enrichment tool that it is, I hope to see you in one of our Leader Certification Courses this year. As Corrie ten Boom wisely states, "Don't bother to give God instructions. Just report for duty." It doesn't matter whether you are a Marine in uniform or a Marine at heart, you should know your mission. If you can't decide on one, I suggest that you read *A Message to Garcia* by Elbert Hubbard and learn the process!

The Power of Thought

Dr. Napoleon Hill

Man is the only creature on earth with the power of self-determination, the right to choose what his thoughts and actions will be. Animals of a lower order are governed by six inherent habits and instincts and do not possess the power to understand situations, except in the simplest acts of existence such as detecting the presence of food by its smell, or finding a way out of a maze by bumping their heads against a wall until an opening is found. The distinguishing characteristic of the human species is its ability to think. Man possesses one thing over which he has the inherent, absolute right of control, and that is his mental attitude. The very idea of man's having absolute control over his thoughts is tremendous. It shows unmistakably a close relationship between the mind of man and Infinite Intelligence. The implications of this simple statement of fact are awe-inspiring. Management of the mind is the key to both the power of our own subconscious mind, and the power of Infinite Intelligence. In the final analysis it means that any plan or purpose which man can conceive in his conscious mind, he can fulfill, either to his benefit, edification, improvement and joy, or to his misery, degradation and ultimate destruction.

PMA Science of Success Course, Educational Edition. Napoleon Hill Foundation, 1961, p. 31.

CHAPTER 20

The majority of students ACCI works with are inner-city youth whose exposure to career options are limited and their environment is not always a positive influence. Think and Grow Rich is a book that will show these students that anyone from anywhere can accomplish any dream with determination and a positive attitude, which is exactly what ACCI Founder Oscar Harris did.

— H. Lee Jarboe

Norman Vincent Peale states, "Any fact facing us is not as important as our attitude toward it, for that determines our success or failure." I agree with this statement, but I like to couple it with the one by Napoleon Hill that adds the extra dimension that many people forget. Hill reminds us that, "It is always your next move." The crucial word here is move, or in another word, action. Being positive or negative is a good starting point, but it does not win us the race.

The odds are stacked in our favor when we can consistently maintain a positive mental attitude, but the winning cup goes to the people who take the required action in life's race, and put their attitude into motion. When given an opportunity, do you take the risk? You better, because a person cannot grow without risk taking. Many people are fearful of stepping out and taking a risk that could turn out to be the chance of a lifetime. Rather, they opt for security and miss the life that they could have lived. This is what Henry David Thoreau calls a life of quiet desperation. We all know that the ultimate outcome in each of our lives is death, but the question is not whether we will die, it is whether we will decide to live. And, yes, the decision is ours, and ours alone.

Begin to accept life's challenges, risks, and opportunities as doorways leading to a new and improved life. Sign up for the class you are uncertain will make a difference, attend a dinner that you would rather miss, listen to an audio program outside your area of immediate interest, take a trip with a friend because the friend feels you will enjoy it, even though you don't expect to. Just show up and see what bountiful opportunities the Universe places on your doorstep every single day. It might be a daisy, a cat, a rainstorm, or the newspaper that appears unexpectedly, but appreciate it as it was meant for you. I wonder what risks you will accept today? Could it be that the risk you embrace is really the invitation to a new and improved version of the life you currently live? Why not see what happens by answering "yes" when you would rather say "no." That is the purpose of having a positive mental attitude. Practice saying "yes," and then follow through.

Mental Attitude Can Be Negative or Positive

Dr. Napoleon Hill

Only a positive mental attitude pays off in the affairs of our everyday living, so let us see what it is, and how we may get it and apply it in the struggle for the things and circumstances we desire in life.

A positive mental attitude has many facets and innumerable combinations for its application in connection with every circumstance which affects our lives.

First of all, a positive mental attitude is the fixed purpose to make every experience, whether it is pleasant or unpleasant, yield some form of benefit which will help us to balance our lives with all the things which lead to peace of mind.

It is the habit of searching for the "seed of an equivalent benefit" which comes with every failure, defeat, or adversity we experience, and causing that seed to germinate into something beneficial. Only a positive mental attitude can recognize and benefit by the lessons or the seed of an equivalent benefit which comes with all unpleasant things that one experiences.

A positive mental attitude is the habit of keeping the mind busily engaged in connection with the circumstances and things one desires in life, and off the things one does not desire. The majority of people go all the way through life with their mental attitudes dominated by fears and anxieties and worries over circumstances which somehow have a way of making their appearance sooner or later. And the strange part of this truth is that these people often blame other people for the misfortunes they have thus brought upon themselves by their negative mental attitudes.

You Can Work Your Own Miracles. Random House, 1971, pp. 11–12.

CHAPTER 21

The number one cause of divorce, depression, and dissatisfaction in our society is reported to be worry over money matters. I've got to believe that the majority of the worry is not about retirement, college education, or paying off the house. Most worries are about those routine, daily matters that come to us unexpectedly and can only be resolved with money.

– Jim Stovall

It's always good to look at your bank balance and know that money is available for unexpected expenses. These funds might be termed rainy day funds or called something else, but in essence they are the monies that you can rely on when a need arises. Just knowing that this money is available will help you sleep better at night. There is nothing worse than wondering where your next dime will come from or how you can acquire funds if the need suddenly arises. Whether it is a death in the family, an accident, the failure of an appliance, or an unexpected tax bill, you can literally rest assured if you have put some funds away for this "rainy day." Knowing that you need this capital, and then cultivating the art of saving regularly can alleviate a potential financial disaster. So, for a financial need, the solution might be as simple as self-discipline and sacrifice until the goal is reached.

On the other hand, do you have an emotional and spiritual bank balance that you can draw from too in the time of greatest need? Financial savings can give you a certain peace of mind, but there is far more to life than a hefty bank balance. Ask yourself who you would turn to for support or assistance if something happened that could not be fixed by money. What friendships do you have that would serve you in a time of emotional or spiritual need? If you have a huge deficit in this area, how do you grow this account? In the end, those individuals you can turn to with a life problem and receive an open door greeting are the people who contribute to your emotional solvency. These people are worth their weight in gold.

To cultivate this process, as with finances you must care for and feed budding relationships. Friendships are not one-sided. If you are on either the giving or the receiving end, you must make sure that a balance exists in the relationship. Out of balance relationships can exist, but not for long. By being both a giver and a receiver you maintain an equilibrium that doesn't drift too far off center. It is in the doing that the connection is maintained and established. Are you a doer or a dreamer? Doers are rewarded by having "karma" credited to their accounts, dreamers only have the promise of future earnings. By this I mean that in order to justify requesting assistance from someone you must first do something to deserve it. It is in the doing that we are entitled to receive. So, have you called or visited a friend? Have you done something unsolicited for another? Have you shared what you have in a spirit of generosity? Have you given to give and not given to get? Try this process on for size. For a calendar month, do something each day without the expectation of compensation from the recipient or anyone else. After the month is up, mentally check your emotional/spiritual bank balance. You will be surprised at the goodness that you have spread around, and in so doing you have enhanced your positivity, one good act at a time.

And, you will be making a difference, both for another and yourself.

Think and Grow Rich
and Peace of Mind

Dr. Napoleon Hill

My book *Think and Grow Rich* has been read by perhaps seven million men and women. In the twenty years since it was published I have been able to talk to some of these people, and I see that some have used the book to help them become rich in money only. It is time to set down once more the twelve great riches of life:

1. A positive mental attitude
2. Sound physical health
3. Harmony in human relationships
4. Freedom from all forms of fear
5. The hope of future achievement
6. The capacity for faith
7. A willingness to share one's blessings
8. A labor of love as an occupation
9. An open mind on all subjects
10. Self-discipline in all circumstances
11. The capacity to understand others
12. Sufficient money

These are the riches which can and should go along with peace of mind. Notice I have set money in the last place, and this despite my insisting that it is very difficult to have peace of mind without sufficient money. I set it there because you yourself will automatically give emphasis to money. Now and then, therefore, I must remind you to de-emphasize it and remember this: Money will buy a great deal but it will not buy peace of mind—it only will help you find peace of mind. But neither money nor anything else can help you find peace of mind unless you begin the journey from within yourself.

Grow Rich! With Peace of Mind. Ballantine, 1996, pp. 67–68.

CHAPTER 22

Self-awareness is crucial to banishing thought vampires that interfere with realizing definite purpose. As I become more aware of my counterproductive thoughts, I transcend being victimized by them. It's deeply empowering to know we all have the ability to choose life-giving thoughts and the subsequent actions that support the fulfillment of our heartfelt desires.

— Catherine Lenard

If you can't control your mind, who will? Are you willing to abdicate control of your greatest asset to someone or something else? It would be like giving away the safety deposit box because you are too ashamed to admit that you have lost the key! Mind control is not magical, other worldly, or occult. It is sheer discipline that keeps you on the path to the specific end result you seek. The recipe is persistence, practice, and patience with yourself in working toward any goal.

Negative self-talk creeps into our positive mindset when we allow it to enter. Low self-esteem, lack of rest, unhealthy lifestyle, and many other causes can contribute to negativity assuming a major role. Like weeds in a garden, these thoughts must be identified and then removed. Whether it is with a shovel or an affirmation, negativity must be pulled up by it roots.

Opposites exist in this world and are beneficial because without experiencing the bad, how would we recognize the good? Without sunlight, who would appreciate the shade? Knowing that there are two sides to every coin—heads and tails—makes us consider our choices. By looking for the silver lining we condition ourselves to go towards the good. By conditioning our minds, we can also train ourselves to focus on the end result we want to attain. Use your mind to create the life than you want to live —yes, you can think and grow rich!

Without thinking there is no progress, and without positive change, there is no richness in life. Learn to use the subtle power of your mind's influence, and always go for the gold! But, also recognize that nothing gold can stay permanently. Therefore, life's experiences are conditions and you do the conditioning every single day with the thoughts you hold in your mind. Therein is the real gold. That is what you can take to the bank. Its value? Priceless.

How Can One Control the Mental Attitude?

Dr. Napoleon Hill

The starting point of control of the mental attitude is motive and desire. No one ever does anything without a motive, or motives, and the stronger the motive the easier it is to control the mental attitude.

Mental attitude can be influenced and controlled by a number of factors, such as:

1. By a BURNING DESIRE for the attainment of a definite purpose based upon one or more of the nine basic motives which activate all human endeavor.

2. By conditioning the mind to automatically choose and carry out definite positive objectives, with the aid of the EIGHT GUIDING PRINCES, or some similar technique which will keep the mind busily engaged with positive objectives, when one is asleep as well as when one is awake.

3. By close association with people who inspire active engagement in positive purposes, and refusal to be influenced by negative-minded people.

4. By auto-suggestion through which the mind is constantly given positive directives until it attracts only that for which these directives call.

5. By a profound recognition, through its adoption and use, of the individual's exclusive privilege of controlling and directing his own mind.

6. By the aid of a machine by which the subconscious mind can be given definite directives while one sleeps.

You Can Work Your Own Miracles. Ballantine, 1996, pp. 15–16.

CHAPTER 23

The last four years of my life have been trying, but this has taught me that the application of all 17 of Napoleon Hill's principles is a powerful blend. Like any recipe, each ingredient lends itself to the whole without giving itself totally up. Each principle likewise lends itself to the whole without giving itself totally up.

– Michael Frain

Napoleon Hill states, "If you can keep on trying after three failures in a given undertaking you may consider yourself a 'suspect' as a potential leader in your chosen occupation. If you can keep on trying after a dozen failures the seed of a genius is germinating within your soul."

These seeds that grow into full blown leadership are only germinated through action. Once you have selected the seeds that are given to you cleverly packaged within the adversity and defeat that you have experienced, it is then that you yourself must decide whether you take the action to plant and cultivate them into the success that you imagine. Once this decision is reached the Law of Cosmic Habitforce comes into play and the seed germinates and is incubated in darkness before it sees the light of day.

Recently I had a challenge in renewing my driver's license due to my name not matching other forms of ID. When the error occurred, I pointed it out to the agency that issued the license but they refused to modify it. So, now almost a decade of renewals later, I was denied my license. On the second visit, I came armed with multiple forms of ID that indicated my "correct" name and not the abbreviated form. I was prepared and determined to have my license processed correctly before I left since I had no more time to devote to it. With a stack of papers that included my passport, tax returns, current billings, etc., I approached the agent and indicated immediately that I had brought in everything I had except my death certificate, and I came to renew my license. With that being said, she knew I wasn't leaving without it, and within the time it took to copy my paperwork I had my license renewal for five years. Success!

The seed in this adversity is that now my official license matches my passport and my social security card. When I need those documents again in the future for processing they will all match and the process will be streamlined. Had I gone back to the bureau that created the misprint, I would still be in line arguing that it was their fault not mine. But, given the information needed to correct the error, I gathered the documents and armed myself with what I needed. Result—application was accepted and processed days before my license expired. And, I feel like a 16-year-old in the fact that I accomplished something bureaucratic without losing my drive to get the job done.

So, action as always is the key to success. When the seed of renewal is in the incubation stage, action is needed to force the seedling into the light of day. Once you believe it you will see it and only then will you rejoice in the bloom that is your reward for your persistence in getting the job done.

Blessing or Curse

Dr. Napoleon Hill

Failure is a blessing or a curse, depending upon the individual's reaction to it. If one looks upon failure as a sort of nudge from the Hand of Destiny which signals him to move in another direction, and if he acts upon that signal, the experience is practically sure to become a blessing. If he accepts failure as an indication of his weakness and broods over it until it produces an inferiority complex, then it is a curse. The nature of the reaction tell the story, and this is under the exclusive control of the individual always.

No one has complete immunity against failure, and everyone meets with failure many times during a lifetime, but everyone also has the privilege and the means by which he can react to failure in any manner he pleases.

Circumstances over which one has no control may, and they sometimes do, result in failure, but there are no circumstances which can prevent one from reacting to failure in a manner best suited for his benefit.

Failure is an accurate measuring device by which an individual may determine his weaknesses; and it provides therefore an opportunity for correcting them. In this sense failure always is a blessing.

You Can Work Your Own Miracles. Ballantine, 1996, pp. 89–90.

CHAPTER 24

Napoleon Hill wrote that everyone has an imagination. They just don't put it to use. What a shame! Studies show that 90 percent of us are visual. We can only see what is there in front of us. Why is that? Because we do not put our imagination to the test.

– Donna Green Sikorski

Have you ever considered words that tickle your fancy and inspire you too? Off the top of my head I will list ten words that I find intriguing. Here they are: *eccentric, gypsy, starship, coincidence, circle, faith, blossoms, lionhearted, creative,* and *vagabond.* By just saying and reading these words I am able to heighten my senses and propel my imagination beyond my normal limits.

Next, read as I attempt to put these words into a sentence. Here goes:

The vagabond gypsy used her creative imagination and envisioned a starship filled with eccentric lifeforms comprised of circular blossoms that coincidentally resembled the lionhearted faith she possessed in her ability to foretell the future.

Crazy, huh? Okay, now you try it. Off the top of your head list ten words that appeal to you and next author a sentence that utilizes all of these words. Now, ponder on what you have done. What have you drawn out of your creative imagination now that may be waiting to be tapped? Chances are you will not write the most profound sentence or grammatically correct sentence, but something will stand in front of you as you read what you have written on your paper. Perhaps, this could be your "higher self" that Dr. Hill discusses in his writings. Coax your imagination and creative ability forward by using techniques such as this one that allow you to drift back into your mind's depths and extract something that may be waiting to be brought into the light.

Perhaps, I should research gypsies and explore their backgrounds and lifestyles. Maybe I should write a story about the life of a vagabond. Or, maybe I should take a crystal ball in hand, tie a sash around my waist and a scarf around my hair, and have a ready made Halloween persona that I can explore as an alternate personality. Whatever idea or feeling ensues, follow it to the end and utilize it to prod your creative imagination forward. Only you know where it can lead. As you bait the hook, expect a big catch.

Ships at anchor are safe, or so the saying goes, but we all know that is not what ships are made for. Set sail and discover new lands and interests within your uncharted self. I wonder what new country you will discover!

Be Your Own Master

Dr. Napoleon Hill

Cherish your visions and your dreams. They are the children of your soul, the blueprints of your ultimate achievements.

The Creator made you a creature who can think for himself, be himself, believe in what he wishes to accomplish, and mightily achieve! Do less than this and you cannot possibly fulfill yourself in all your glorious humanity.

The mind of man is filled with powers to be used, not to be neglected. These powers, these blessings, either are used—and the benefits of their use shared with others—or you incur penalties for not using them.

If you needed a house, and knew how to build a house, and had all the materials you needed for building a house, and had a lot on which to build a house, and yet neglected to build a house—then you would understand your penalty as you sat exposed in the rain and the snow.

Too many of us do not use our power to gather in the wealth and peace of mind which is available all around us. Then we are penalized by poverty, by misery, by worry and ill health—and we blame everyone but ourselves.

Anything the human mind can believe, the human mind can achieve.

Believe in poverty and you will be poor.
Believe in wealth and you will be rich.
Believe in love and you will have love.
Believe in health and you will be healthy.

Grow Rich! With Peace of Mind. Ballantine, 1996, p. 234.

CHAPTER 25

Farmers are a wonderful example of individuals who apply themselves at the crack of dawn, when the rooster crows, and retire when the sun sets. One of the reasons is because they have to work with nature, where standards and principles are set in divine order. The other reason is simply because of the love and joy of what nature has to offer each day.

– Loretta Levin

Napoleon Hill writes, "The power of the seventeen principles consists not in the principles, but in their application and use! When the principles are applied they change the 'chemistry' of the mind from a negative to a positive mental attitude. It is this positive mental attitude which attracts success by leading one to the attainment of the Twelve Riches." Dr. Hill goes on to add that the principles may be likened to the letters of the alphabet through the combination of which we express our thoughts.

Consider applying the "alphabet" to the habit of going the extra mile. Begin with the letter "A" and on a sheet of loose-leaf paper next to the letter write down something you will do beginning with the letter "A" that causes you to go the extra mile. Next, follow through with the other 25 letters. Begin with an action word and when finished with your list, take immediate action on the tasks you have just established for yourself.

Here is a five-step list in alphabetical order to get you started in setting up your office space:

- Arrange my desk in an easily accessible fashion
- Build a desktop file that sorts my daily work
- Communicate daily tasks verbally to co-workers
- Divide "to-do" lists into important/unimportant
- Energize myself by moving around every hour

You get the idea. Now begin by building some tasks that focus on establishing a productive routine for what it is you want to do in ABC order. Continue to brainstorm with yourself until the list is complete.

Another method to utilize after completing the task at hand is to simply ask your "higher self" what should be done next? You will always receive an immediate answer. The result is in the doing—the completion of the task, not in overly analyzing it or thinking about it.

These simple games will get you started, and soon these self-starters become habits that will serve you well for the rest of your life.

The Advantages of the Habit of Going the Extra Mile

Dr. Napoleon Hill

The habit brings the individual to the favorable attention of those who can and will provide opportunities for self-advancement.

- It tends to make one indispensable, in many different human relationships, and it therefore enables him to command more than average compensation for personal services.

- It leads to mental growth and to physical skill and perfection in many forms of endeavor, thereby adding to one's earning capacity.

- It protects one against the loss of employment when employment is scarce, and places him in a position to command the choicest of jobs.

- It enables one to profit by the law of contrast, since the majority of people do not practice the habit.

- It leads to the development of a positive, pleasing mental attitude, which is essential for enduring success.

- It tends to develop a keen, alert imagination because it is a habit which inspires one continuously to seek new and better ways of rendering service.

- It develops the important quality of personal initiative.

- It develops self-reliance and courage.

- It serves to build the confidence of others in one's integrity.

- It aids in the mastery of the destructive habit of procrastination.
- It develops definiteness of purpose, insuring one against the common habit of aimlessness.

The Master-Key to Riches. Fawcett Crest, 1965, pp. 60–61.

CHAPTER 26

The labyrinth is a pattern that has been used for thousands of years as a kinesthetic form of meditation. Your body and mind open as you walk a unicursal path. Taking time out to meditate may just give you a transforming "a-ha!" moment in which everything must change or rearrange to accommodate a vision or inspiration received.

— Uriel Martinez

Dr. Hill states that Creative Vision is the product of a well-defined purpose and has at its base the spirit of the universe which expresses itself through us. He adds that Creative Vision recognizes no such thing as the regularity of working hours, is not concerned with monetary compensation, and its highest aim is to do the impossible. Wow! What a compliment when someone says that you are creative! Taking all of the above into account, if you are creative, that makes you nothing short of a miracle worker!

Creativity demands respect. When the creator—little "c"—begins to work on a project, the rest of us must stand aside and let the Creator—big "C"—do the work through the individual doing the project, or even ourselves if we are the creator. For example, cooking involves creativity. Not just in the preparation of the dish, but in the selection of the recipe, in the creation of the recipe first in our mind, and then in reality. Creativity is work—just not work that is immediately visible. Each of us can be creative—we are hardwired for it from birth—but we may have to experiment to find our best creative medium.

All work can be creative. Whether you are an artist, a chef, a seamstress, a gardener, a musician, a writer, or anything else—creativity is your imagination at work. Use this innate human talent to your benefit.

First, conceive it, second, believe it, and third, achieve it! Creativity always works from the inside out. Dr. Hill reminds us that "Creative Vision is developed by the free and fearless use of one's imagination." Our job is to put creativity into practice within the realm of our existing talents gifted to us by the Creator at birth. Essentially, we are given the gift, and it is our task on earth to find out how best to utilize this gift within our life. Start now, and watch the miraculous results unfold.

The Spirit of the Universe

Dr. Napoleon Hill

Creative vision extends beyond interest in material things. It judges the future by the past, and concerns itself with the future more than with the past. Imagination is influenced and controlled by the powers of reason and experience. Creative vision pushes both of these aside and attains its ends basically by new ideas and methods.

While imagination recognizes limitations, handicaps and opposition, creative vision rides over these as if they did not exist and arrives at its destination. Imagination is seated in the intellect of man. Creative vision has its base in the spirit of the universe which expresses itself through the brain of man.

PMA Science of Success Course, Educational Edition. Napoleon Hill Foundation, 1961, p. 411.

CHAPTER 27

Most people grasp rather quickly that if they procrastinate, they put things off, and then they want to cure themselves of this habit; I recommend that they memorize the three words—Do it Now—and repeat those three words fifty times in the morning, fifty times at night, with enthusiasm and with rapidity, for a week or ten days until it's so ingrained in the subconscious mind in time of need; then when it does, a person immediately gets into action.

— *W. Clement Stone*

The French psychologist Émile Coué gave the world a very simple formula for maintaining a sound health consciousness. He recommended the daily repetition of this sentence:

"Every day in every respect, I am getting better and better." Once the subconscious mind picks up the message and acts on it, the result is good health. The opposite side of the coin is the statement, "If you think you are sick, you are."

Which one do you want to adopt? Our mind cannot hold two competing thoughts at once. The predominating thought is the one that literally impresses our subconscious mind and brings about the involuntary powerful actions that produce the changes on a cellular level. If we remember the simple phrase, thoughts are things, we know internally that what we think about we become.

I am often amazed how people line up for a diagnosis of what ails them, but fail to become proactive in their treatment plan. Disease begins invisibly on a subtle level at first. By the time diagnosis is reached, a person has a lot of backtracking to do in order to reverse the process. Why not begin with preventative mechanisms? These "treatments" can be as simple as guided imagery, relaxation, meditation, massage, aromatherapy, walking, proper nutrition, etc. If you take personal initiative and begin to heal when the problem is maybe just a thought of distress, you won't have to bother with a medical diagnosis. Control your thoughts, control your emotions, and thereby control your destiny! Think *healthy*, *happy*, and *terrific* thoughts day by day.

Autosuggestion

Dr. Napoleon Hill

Autosuggestion is the medium through which every individual stimulates his mind continuously. Unfortunately most of the stimuli which ready the mind of the average person by self-suggestion are of a negative nature. They consist of thoughts of the conditions and things which one does not want—fears, worries, hatreds, envy, greed and superstition.

The most successful person uses autosuggestion as a medium for feeding his mind with the thoughts of things and circumstances he desires, including a health consciousness.

Take notice of the principle of autosuggestion and ponder it carefully, for it is the common carrier which may bring sound health or may bring illness. It is the medium by which the hypochondriac poisons his own mind from within by belief in ailments which do not exist except in his own mind.

Take notice of autosuggestion also, because it is the principle through which one may convey to his subconscious mind a clear picture of his definite major purpose in life.

Religion—regardless of its sectarian brand—is a mind stimulant of the highest and noblest order. There are no negative reactions to belief in Infinite Intelligence and it is a builder of sound physical health without an equal.

Eat right, think right, sleep right, and play right, and you can save the doctor's bill for your vacation money.

When the world is truly civilized, religion will dominate all human relationships. It will go with a man to his job and it will sustain him in his home while he plays. It will be his guide seven days a week, and he will not only believe it, but he will live by it! He will live by the creed of what is right.

PMA Science of Success Course, Educational Edition. Napoleon Hill Foundation, 1961, p. 456.

CHAPTER 28

*From a career healing those with injury and disease, I know
all too well how life can be unbalanced. So many of us equate
healing with doctors and hospitals, not realizing we have the
power within us to change our realities. Self-healing is available to all of us at any time; we simply have to have faith
and act.*

— Laura Dietrich-Lake

L ife is too short to have devastating setbacks from which
one cannot recover. Have you ever had one or *thought* you
had one?

I can guess that the majority of readers today have responded
with a big *"yes!"* to both questions. Whether real or imaginary,
each one of us has experienced bad things that have obscured all
hope of recovery while we are locked in the experience. In order
to recover and move ahead, it is required that a true out-of-body
experience occurs. By this I mean that we have to force movement within ourselves to get over, beyond, around, or through
what has temporarily shackled us. This requires action, and the
sooner action is taken the better. Only action will propel us into
another time and space. Navel-gazing needs to be replaced with
stargazing so that we can advance to become the higher selves
that Dr. Hill discusses.

Recently I saw a sign that stated, "Don't look back. You're not headed in that direction." In two short sentences we are reminded that life should be future focused, not past encumbered. If we "live" in the past, we are missing the present and what gifts the present holds for us. I believe that the past should be honored for what contribution it has made in creating our current reality, but if we stay stuck there nothing new will transpire in our lives.

Just as the butterfly leaves the cacoon transformed, so too we are leaving our past more magnificent for having experienced it.

A Prescription for Success

Dr. Napoleon Hill

Education, skill and experience are useful assets in every calling, but they will be of little value to the man who, like the Arab of the desert, folds up his tent and silently steals away when he is defeated. The man with a definite major purpose, faith and determination may occasionally be swept from the success side of the River of Life by circumstances beyond his control, but he will not long remain there. For his mental reaction to his defeat will be sufficiently strong to carry him back to the success side where he rightfully belongs.

Failure and adversity have introduced many men to opportunities which they would not have recognized under more favorable circumstances.

A man's mental attitude in respect to defeat is the factor of major importance in determining whether he rides with the tides of fortune on the success side of the River of Life or is swept to the failure side by circumstances of misfortune.

The circumstances which separate failure from success often are so slight that their real cause is overlooked. Often they exist entirely in the mental attitude with which one meets temporary defeat. The man with a positive mental attitude reacts to defeat in a spirit of determination to accept it. The man with a negative mental attitude reacts to defeat in a spirit of hopeless acceptance.

PMA Science of Success Course, Educational Edition. Napoleon Hill Foundation, 1961, p. 395–396.

CHAPTER 29

It doesn't matter how small you were when you first came into this world. What matters is how much you grow each day of your life. It takes great self-discipline to act each day in a way that allows you to grow spiritually, intellectually, economically, and socially.

— *Virginia Ward*

Summer's abundance is upon us and I am continually amazed at nature's prolific output. I have a dwarf peach tree that this year alone produced over 700 peaches. Within that harvest is contained the seeds for an orchard of peach trees. And, inside the apple that I ate for lunch today are embedded nearly 15 seeds that when planted can produce an overabundance of apples. Amazing.

When we look closely, we can always detect the macrocosm in the microcosm. The orchard hidden in a single apple, the peach grove produced by a single peach tree, and the goodness we do for another achieving a broader application. Herein resides one of the most profound mysteries of the universe. What we do for others not only comes back to us as a reciprocal blessing or curse, but also has the capacity to change the world. It's like the magic in the seed.

Many times most of us feel that what we do does not matter. We take both goodness and evil for granted and begin to believe that our thoughts and actions do not make a significant difference. Nothing could be further from the truth. The energy in both thought and action that we set into motion within our small world changes not only us but those near and far. In creating our little world, we are also co-creating the larger world around us.

Whether it's ripples that replicate in a pond, a sound that reverberates in a beat, or a tender reassuring pat on the hand, all our actions produce more than we can imagine. We need to have extrasensory perception in order to look beyond the commonplace.

Granted, it's difficult to track the path of every thought and action that emanates from us, but it would be beneficial if we could. Just by knowing how swift our thoughts and actions can transform ourselves and others might cause us to consider outcomes first. Think before we speak. Look. Listen. Be careful. When we realize that what we put out there is contagious, we first must consider whether or not it is something that should be caught!

Your Magnificent Obsession

Dr. Napoleon Hill & W. Clement Stone

The more you share, the more you will have. Now if you doubt this, you can prove it to yourself by giving: a smile to everyone you meet; a kind word; a pleasant response; appreciation with warmth from the heart; cheer; encouragement; hope; honor, credit, and applause; good thoughts; evidence of love for your fellowmen; happiness; a prayer for the godless and the godly; and time for a worthy cause with eagerness.

If you do experiment by giving any one of the above, you will also prove to yourself what we have found is one of the most difficult principles to teach those who need it most: how to cause desirable actions within yourself. Until you do learn, you will fail to realize that what is left with you when you share it with others will multiply and grow; and what you withhold from others will diminish and decrease. Therefore, share that which is good and desirable and withhold that which is bad and undesirable.

Success Through a Positive Mental Attitude. Prentice-Hall, 1960, pp. 165–166.

CHAPTER 30

When we take time to pause and write down our thoughts we can see what kind of attitude we have. How often are we positive or negative concerning specific subjects? How automatic our responses have become concerning certain subjects?

— *Uriel Martinez*

A popular song by the Bee Gees is entitled, "It's Only Words." The lyrics in that song state: *It's only words / And words are all I have / To take your heart away.* How often have our words been just the opposite of the sentiment implied in that song? Words can harm, and words can heal. Criticism far exceeds praise when it comes to attempting to motivate someone, and yet research tells us that criticism does not work. In fact, criticism may not only cause a stalemate or a standstill, but can negatively intensify the situation. What's a person to do when language alone is an ineffective form of communication?

One idea is to observe the words we use when communicating with others. For communication to occur, there must be a speaker and a listener. Both parties need to be engaged in the process and be open to honest communication. Without receptivity and feedback, no thought is really exchanged. Someone who fails to respond, or simply withholds comment, is not communicating. Give and take is essential in a conversation. It cannot be one-sided. We've all heard the complaint, "I might as well be talking to the wall." More often than not, many of us have felt this way when there is a breakdown in communication. Perhaps our own words need a makeover. Maybe there is too much "I" and not enough "We." Maybe the words connote or denote something unpleasant to the listener. Maybe our vocabulary needs refinement.

Positive Mental Attitude vocabulary does not allow toxic words as choices. This is not to say that these words do not exist, but that it is a person's conscious choice not to use them. Just as we have an ecological footprint due to the manner in which we practice living "green," so too can we have a PMA footprint. The saying goes, "What you think about, you bring about." Even more so, what you verbalize can actually take you footprint by footprint, step by step, toward or away from your ultimate goal. Which way are you traveling?

How to Energize Your Subconscious Mind for Creative Effort

Dr. Napoleon Hill

For the present, it is sufficient if you remember that you are living daily, in the midst of all manner of thought impulses which are reaching your subconscious mind, without your knowledge. Some of these impulses are negative, some are positive. You are now engaged in trying to help shut off the flow of negative impulses, and to aid in voluntarily influencing your subconscious mind, through positive impulses of desire.

When you achieve this, you will possess the key which unlocks the door to your subconscious mind. Moreover, you will control that door so completely, that no undesirable thought may influence your subconscious mind.

Everything which man creates begins in the form of a thought impulse. Man can create nothing which he does not first conceive in thought. Through the aid of the imagination, thought impulses may be assembled into plans. The imagination, when under control, may be used for the creation of plans or purposes that lead to success in one's chosen occupation.

All thought impulses, intended for transmutation into their physical equivalent, voluntarily planted in the subconscious mind, must pass through the imagination, and be mixed with faith. The "mixing" of faith with plan, or purpose, intended for submission to the subconscious mind, may be done only through the imagination.

From these statements, you will readily observe that voluntary use of the subconscious mind calls for coordination and application of all the principles.

Think and Grow Rich. Ballantine, 1960, p. 179.

CHAPTER 31

How can you think long term, build internal symbols with harmony in your life and your business? How can you build this vision in your company and make this process a competitive advantage in today's world? This alliance requires harmony, a well-defined vision, and an "army" of mental advisors such as gratitude, faith, love, behavior, hope, patience and wisdom.

— Jamil Albuquerque

Mastermind Alliance allows participants to work in perfect harmony for the common good of the group's goal. Most jobs in life are not handled by single persons. Everyone knows something, but a single person cannot know or do everything. To be successful, all a person needs to do is become an expert in an area of choosing. This is possible to do. However, in order to master one certain trade or technique, the other opportunities must become roads not taken. To do one thing very well is an art, to do many things with equal expertise is highly improbable and impractical. Things we are not accustomed to do or not qualified to do are best delegated or shared with others. Whether it's dentistry, surgery, therapy, or something else, most people need a mastermind of sorts for these and other services.

In maintaining our outer life, we use services to assist us in getting jobs done. According to Dr. Hill, our inner life can be the same. If we had to oversee the functioning of our physical systems, we would be occupied all day with blood circulation, digestion, breathing, elimination, etc. However, we do not have to do this because our autonomic nervous system does this for us. Breathing, for example, is not something we have to remind ourselves to do on each in breath or out breath. It happens spontaneously. And, when it doesn't, it becomes all we can think about.

Dr. Hill feels it is a worthwhile idea to consciously put designated "princes" in charge of things we ourselves cannot directly attend to or control ourselves. For example, the Prince of Peace of Mind's duty is to keep the mind free from all forms of fear and causes of worry. The Prince of Sound Health's duty is to keep the physical body healed and efficient at all times. In this regard, we free ourselves from extraneous concerns that could deplete our creative thoughts through surveillance and worry alone.

I think it is a reasonable idea to direct our thoughts to a "prince" in charge and ask him to mind the store in a manner of speaking so we don't have to. This then informs our conscious mind that we are on duty and attending to things. In turn, this removes our mind from the mundane and frees us up for higher thinking without feeling neglectful. My advice is, if it works—use it!

How To Make Practical Use of the Master Mind Compact

Dr. Napoleon Hill

1. Relate yourself to the nine invisible guides precisely as if they were real people in the flesh, and talk to them in the same friendly tone of voice as you would talk to personal friends.

2. Express your gratitude to the guides at the close of each day, just before retiring, thanking each one individually for the service you have received today, the service that the Guide will render you while you sleep, and the service that will be rendered you tomorrow.

3. Before beginning any plan or the pursuit of any aim or purpose ask the Guides to condition your mind for successful termination of your activity, and thank them in advance for having blessed you with success.

4. When you are in doubt regarding any plan or purpose you may have in mind, before reaching a decision request the Guide of Over-all Wisdom to give you directions.

5. Before engaging in any sort of negotiation with other people in connection with your occupation, business or profession, request your Guides to condition the mind of those with whom you contemplate such relationship so they will be favorable to you. (If you are engaged in any form of selling, this habit, if sincerely adhered to, will work miracles for you.)

6. BELIEVE that all requests you make of your Guides will be granted, that all services you request of them will be rendered. (But be careful not to request of them any

form of service which would injure another person, or cause another person a loss of any nature whatsoever.)

7. The Guiding Princes work only for gratitude, therefore express your gratitude to them both before and after they serve you.

8. This Master-Mind Compact gives you the privilege of tuning in on the success beam of Napoleon Hill, therefore end all of your requests for services by the Guides by an expression of gratitude for this privilege.

9. The results you will experience from the Master Mind alliance with Napoleon Hill will become noticeable in exact proportion to your development of FAITH in its efficacy.

10. The principle upon which the Master-Mind Compact is based is scientifically sound and it does not interfere, in any manner whatsoever, with anyone's religious beliefs, since the essence of it is based on FAITH, and the power of FAITH is an accepted essential in all religions.

Unpublished article from the Napoleon Hill Archives, Hammond, IN.

CHAPTER 32

Self-motivators are the key to "The Success System That Never Fails." Each is either a statement of fact or a command. They have already affected your subconscious mind and will continue to do so every time you repeat them. It would be well to memorize those which you believe can be most meaningful to you.

— W. Clement Stone

Calm minds produce the best results. Worry detracts us from our mission. When we can solely focus on a single event or process we are dedicated to that activity and concentrate our highest thinking skills on getting the task or job done effectively. Time may lose its relevancy too as we move in the eternal flow of the activity without paying attention to clock time. Hours may pass that seem like minutes, and sometimes within minutes we can achieve what would have taken us hours previously had we been multitasking.

One trick that I like to use when my "monkey mind" won't allow me to concentrate solely on one activity, is to entertain it by keeping a list of ideas or thoughts on paper that just won't go away and continue to demand my attention. It might be that I forgot to send a birthday greeting, left the clothes too long at the cleaners, or failed to schedule the next doctor's appointment. I give the thought or idea briefly my attention by jotting it down with the promise of returning later to address it in more detail. This eventually stops as I become more engrossed in what I am doing, and it is a way to alleviate the ever present desire to multitask and in the end accomplish little or nothing. Usually, my attention is divided when I do not enjoy what I am currently required to do. But, I am able to control the impulse to quit and do something more appealing by keeping the list by my side. This tells my other self that distractions and diversions will not work. The goal is to stick to the job until it is done.

Peace of mind does not come without work. In order to capture serenity, silence, and enjoy the eternal now, we must remind ourselves that this is like our eternal fountain of youth. It massages our soul when we give ourselves time to just be. Being is what we are—human beings, not as the saying goes, human doings. With that thought, I wish you just time to be in the moment, be in the present, and give yourself the enjoyable serenity of relaxing in the beauty of each and every precious moment of time we are allotted in the here and now.

Peace of Mind and Power of Mind

Dr. Napoleon Hill

Since what you achieve in life depends on what you first conceive, and this depends first of all upon your deep, inner, subconsciously founded belief—you see that your life depends upon your power to believe.

No, your mere life-processes do not depend upon this power. The Eternal has made it possible for the supreme achievement of evolution, man, to stay alive even without knowing he is alive. The beating of the heart, the pumping of the lungs, the processes of digestion and other vital functions are taken care of by a part of the brain which takes care of itself.

Beyond this, man creates an ever better species. He aspires—and climbs to the heights of his aspiration. Seeing heights yet beyond, again he aspires--and achieves that peak, beyond which lies another and another.

Significantly, philosophers always have recognized the power of the quiet mind, the peaceful mind. This is far from being a mind empty of aspiration. It is, rather, a mind which can hold, judge and evaluate the highest forms of aspiration. Nor is a peaceful mind the exclusive property of a person who does not move about in the world and busy himself with the world's manifold affairs, for some of the most peaceful minds are the busiest. Remember, we speak of inner peace, like a quiet center about which all else revolves, like a great rotating dynamo doing useful work and filled with energy, yet referring its rotation always to the unmoved pivot at its middle.

A mind at peace is a mind that is free to conceive greatly. It bears no great conflict within its subconscious which may hamper the conscious mind and therefore conscious action. A mind at peace is a free mind. Its power is limitless.

Grow Rich! With Peace of Mind. Fawcett, 1967, pp. 203–204.

CHAPTER 33

There is always a seed of equivalent benefit in the face of adversity during difficult periods in our lives. Sometimes it is difficult to see the benefit right away, but it will reveal itself at a later date and time, even years later when you look back on the events. Life's crisis opens the doors for opportunity.

– Dori Naerbo

Ill health is not something any of us hope or wish for in this lifetime. Adjustments or alignments that put us back on track are essential in order to continue to operate at an optimum level. When thinking about health matters we often think about illness when wellness should be our primary focus. The cost of illness should not exceed the cost of wellness. By this I mean that a person should put as much emphasis on staying healthy as he or she does on curing an illness. The saying, "a stitch in time saves nine," can apply to health issues because when something is detected and resolved at the onset, more time can then be focused on maintenance of sound health.

Mental health issues are important ones to consider too. When things seem to be out of the ordinary in our lives, perhaps we are not as tuned in to the everyday give and take that stable mental health requires. A person may be troubled personally, extended financially, touchy emotionally, or reacting in a non-characteristic manner, and this could send up red flags to those who are concerned. Is it depression, hormonal, or something more severe? Being out of sorts for a day or two is one thing, but acting outside of your "normal" personality needs attention before a breach occurs. And, it is in the person's best interest to intervene if they are not able or willing to do it for themselves.

Giving ourselves time to rest, reflect, and renew is crucial in maintaining optimum health. Just by taking daily time to rest and pause before our next assignment gives a person the essential recess that contributes to physical and emotional health. Do yourself a favor. Give yourself those safeguards on a daily basis. Remember that without health, life is much more challenging.

"Un-Peace" of Mind

Dr. Napoleon Hill

In my sixty-odd years of adulthood I have been gratified to see that physicians give increasing attention to psychosomatic illness, or bodily illness which originates in the mind. Since man's earliest history, however, it has been obvious that almost all of our illness is caused by un-peace of mind. Here is a very partial list of symptoms which can arise from mental conflicts, fears, and tensions:

- Headache
- Indigestion
- Ulcers
- Arthritic pains
- Constant fatigue
- Sleeplessness
- Slow healing of wounds
- Kidney trouble
- Circulatory trouble
- Frigidity
- Impotence
- Rashes and other skin afflictions
- Mouth infection
- Rectal disorders
- Muscular cramps
- And more …
- And *more*….

Then there are the many mental disorders, ranging from extreme nervous tension to outright insanity, which often are caused or aggravated by a mind which fights itself. The list of ills to which body and mind may yield is almost endless, so let your first step toward good health be this: do not dwell upon the image of illness. The mind tends to transmute all beliefs into their physical equivalent. Why, then, see yourself as anything but a person who enjoys good sound health from top to toe and back again?

Grow Rich! With Peace of Mind. Fawcett, 1967, pp. 51–52.

CHAPTER 34

*When I started my research on Customer Engagement,
I knew Napoleon Hill's research would play a critical
component in my work and quickly realized that it is
not possible to fully engage customers unless you have an
engaged and empowered workforce.*

– Ray Stendall

Why not challenge yourself to keep a list of books you have read as the weeks go by? I read many books and I think that a list of those that I have read would be as helpful as an official transcript of classes that I have taken. If you are not into reading, but listen to audio books you can use those too. This list would serve a dual purpose.

1. It details the sources of thoughts, ideas, and wisdom you may have gathered from various writers.

2. It allows you to reference a title and author easily if you want to refer the book or audio book to someone else.

Also, if you want to kick your list up a notch, you might indicate the category of book you are reading. Just by going to any library, you can see the various categories that books are shelved in for user access. Generally, this categorization is based upon the Dewey Decimal System or the Library of Congress System for locating books. If your reading is solely in one category such as Fiction, it could mean that you are an expert in that area, or it could also indicate that you are stuck and need to branch out. For example, if you only read Romance Novels, the character names, setting, and plot may change, but generally it is the same story told over and over again. In other words, these books become predictable. Why not challenge yourself to a bigger playing field and read something outside your norm? This type of reading is what enhances your awareness and opens your eyes to new insights.

Below is a list that I compiled over the 17 Success Principles as supplemental reading. You might just benefit from reading one or two of these highly recommended books.

Definiteness of Purpose
Your Greatest Power, J. Martin Kohe
The Artist's Way, Julia Cameron

The Master Mind
Seabiscuit: An American Legend, Laura Hillenbrand

Applied Faith
Believe and Achieve, W. Clement Stone
The Magic of Believing, Claude Bristol
TNT: The Power Within You, Claude Bristol

Going the Extra Mile
Try Giving Yourself Away: A Tonic for These Troubled Times,
David Dunn
The Greatest Salesman in the World, Og Mandino

Pleasing Personality
How To Win Friends and Influence People, Dale Carnegie

Personal Initiative

The Success System that Never Fails, W. Clement Stone
The Alchemist, Paulo Coelho

Positive Mental Attitude

The Power of Positive Thinking, Norman Vincent Peale
Man's Search for Meaning, Viktor Frankl
Love, Medicine and Miracles, Bernie Siegel, MD
Peace, Love and Healing, Bernie Siegel, MD

Enthusiasm

Life Is Tremendous, Charlie "Tremendous" Jones

Self-Discipline

A Message to Garcia, Elbert Hubbard

Accurate Thinking

Key to Yourself, Venice Bloodworth

Controlled Attention

As A Man Thinketh, James Allen

Teamwork

The Wonderful Wizard of Oz, L. Frank Baum

Learning from Adversity and Defeat

Acres of Diamonds, Russell Conwell
The Anatomy of Hope, Jerome Groopman, MD

Creative Vision

Your Word is Your Wand, Florence Scovel Shinn
The Richest Man in Babylon, George Clason

Maintenance of Sound Health

Wake Up! You're Alive, Arnold Fox, MD, and Barry Fox, Ph.D.
Ancient Secret of the Fountain of Youth, Peter Kelder

Budgeting Time and Money
The 7 Habits of Highly Effective People, Stephen Covey

Cosmic Habitforce
The Power of Your Subconscious Mind, Joseph Murphy, Ph.D.

Fresh Thought Needed

Dr. Napoleon Hill

The human mentality withers unless in constant contact with the stimulating influence of fresh thought. The quickest way to break a man's will is to isolate his mind, cutting him off from the books, newspapers, radio and other normal channels of intellectual communication.

Under such circumstances, the intellect dies for lack of nourishment. Only the strongest will and the purest faith can save it. Is it possible that you have imprisoned your mind in a social and cultural concentration camp? Have you subjected yourself to a brain-washing of your own making, isolating you from ideas that could lead to success?

If so, it's time to sweep aside the bars of prejudice that imprison your intellect.

Open your mind and set it free!

Napoleon Hill in the NEWS! Forthcoming from the Napoleon Hill Foundation, January, 2013.

CHAPTER 35

We welcome the warm fuzzies that well up when we think about the good ol' days. Our memories tend to focus more on the good and not so much on the bad. I say let's bring back the good ol' days in whatever way we can.

— Elizabeth Barber

Our thoughts can be affected by many things. The simple smell of a rose, an old photo of a friend, the touch of a baby's blanket, the taste of a favorite comfort food, and the sound of a loved one's voice all elicit emotional feelings that can animate our thoughts. Nostalgia can bring longing for something either near or far, but all sensations of this type have emotional attachments.

For example, when looking at my furniture at home, I have many "nostalgic" or custom pieces that anyone else would call "junk." I admit it. I have an emotional attachment to these pieces. I have a blue table that belonged to my grandfather's twin brother and his wife. This table means a great deal to me because I never met my grandfather. He was gone by the time I arrived. His sister-in-law, my great Aunt Em, gave it to me when she was moving to Florida upon the death of my great-uncle. This table represents part of my family history on my father's side. So, to me it is precious and I would not part with it. Seeing it daily grounds me.

It is good to be aware that sensations can have either positive or negative vibrations. Dr. Hill tells us that when we emotionalize a desire, we can reach our goal sooner because we have intensified, or heightened it. I like to express it this way: Thought + Emotionalized Action = Success. What trips your trigger emotionally? Can you use it to your advantage? Can you express a prayer of gratitude for all the good things in your life that may have come to you over time? Can you see the beauty in the history of something and then simultaneously work to make all things new? Wonder of wonders happens when you can artfully blend the old and the new in order to create an even greater outcome than you expected.

Eternal Change

Dr. Napoleon Hill

Strange also is the fact that only one thing is permanent in this universe-eternal change. Nothing remains exactly the same for even a second. Even the physical body in which we live changes completely with astonishing rapidity.

You can test these statements against your own experience.

When a person is struggling for recognition and to get a few dollars ahead, seldom will he find anyone to give him a needed lift. But once he makes the grade-and no longer needs help-people stand in line to offer him aid.

Through what I call the law of attraction, like attracts like in all circumstances. Success attracts greater success. Failure attracts more failure. Throughout our lives we are the beneficiaries or victims of a swiftly flowing stream which carries us onward toward either success or failure.

The idea is to get on the "success beam" rather than on the "failure beam."

How can you do this? Simple. The answer lies in adopting a positive mental attitude that will help you shape the course of your own destiny rather than drifting along at the mercy of life's adversities.

Napoleon Hill in the NEWS! Forthcoming from the Napoleon Hill Foundation, January, 2013.

CHAPTER 36

Two of the greatest words in our vocabulary are expect
and miracle. *These words awaken the power of expectation
and make possible the enriching qualities of hope, desire,
enthusiasm and excitement that unfold into a rewarding
and purposeful life. By expanding our level of expectation,
we expand and increase our miracles.*

— *John Hinwood*

Blessings are everywhere if only we can train our eyes to see them. Things we take for granted daily in this world are things that are truly miraculous.

Just ask someone who has lost a loved one. Perhaps the miracle of that person's life was not fully appreciated until that person's life ended. It is normal to expect things to remain the same, and when they change, that is when we notice the miracle, sometimes it's too late. Regrets can partially be due to not having tuned in on time to the miracles that surround us.

The practice of meditation causes us to stop our hectic routines and take time to just be. Walking a labyrinth can do this as well. Being in nature and observing the seasonal changes contribute to us entering into a deeper sense of appreciation for the gifts that we are given. This awareness arouses a prayer of thankfulness for being alive and gifted with the beauty of creation.

Writing in a gratitude journal or keeping a list of things to be happy about causes us to focus more on the positive. Otherwise, what tends to monopolize our thoughts are things that create an immediate demand for our attention. There is no end to the "to-do" lists that our minds can create.

But, I like to recall that one of our greatest American philosophers, Benjamin Franklin, reminds us that "moderation in all things" is a good lifestyle to follow. I tend to agree with him. It has been said that if our only tool is a hammer, many things appear to need hammering. By practicing moderation and giving ourselves time to just be, not only are we on the lookout for a calmer approach to living, but we are adding new tools to our holistic toolkit. Hammers have their place, but so do levels, saws, and planes. Each one serves a unique purpose, and in so doing they complement each other. Expect a miracle in your life. The first step in doing so is to strengthen your eyesight so that you recognize one when you see it.

Greatest Blessing

Dr. Napoleon Hill

During the years of research and organization of the Science of Success, I was overtaken by no less than 20 major defeats, each of which provided me with a glorious opportunity to test my capacity for faith. Had it not been for the knowledge revealed to me by these defeats, the Science of Success philosophy could not have been completed during my lifetime.

Perhaps the greatest blessing that came to me through my experiences with defeat was the revelation that prayer can give us guidance, but to benefit by it, we must do something on our own account. Also, the most effective of all our prayers are those which we offer as an expression of gratitude for the blessings we already enjoy, rather than asking for more blessings. After I learned to pray in this way, my blessings began to multiply, until at long last I had everything I desired or needed without having to ask for more.

An important turning point in my life was reached the day I first said, "Oh, Lord, I ask not for more blessings, but for more wisdom with which to make better use of the blessings you gave me at birth—the privilege of controlling and directing my own mind to purposes of my choice." The mind is so designed that it attracts the sum and substance of what one thinks about most often.

As a matter of fact, life brings everyone that which his mind dwells upon, whether his thoughts are based on fear or faith. The majority of people go through life with their mind power directed by fears and self-imposed limitations, and they wonder why life is so unkind to them.

Napoleon Hill in the NEWS! Forthcoming from the Napoleon Hill Foundation, January, 2013.

CHAPTER 37

Not everything in life is straight uphill. You always have to make adjustments. Smart people learn to make adjustments. Sometimes it's hard to keep a positive mental attitude. We're not immune to situations. But if you keep the right attitude, then living in the scope of life is easier.

– David Gilston

Emulating a person you admire is a Napoleon Hill-recommended activity. What you admire in their personality may in time cross over to become one of your very own admirable characteristics.

Seizing upon that one thing that makes a person special in your book can cause you to first notice, second comprehend, and third apply this trait to yourself as you envision yourself becoming. As you structure the "you" you want to become, begin with good ingredients for the very best end result.

David Gilston is a case in point. Early on in his 50-plus year career in insurance sales, he was introduced to *Think and Grow Rich* by none other than W. Clement Stone! Taking Stone's advice to heart, he read the book and followed its directions in creating the very best life he could envision for himself and his family. Today, David continues Stone's legacy by delivering books along with the suggestion that if the contents are followed, you too can become the ultimate success you desire to become.

I met David several years ago on one of our Leader Certification cruises. Quietly, at first, he audited our classes, but by the second day he pronounced the contents sound and the message in line with what

W. Clement Stone himself taught! I was pleased to have passed David's test of authenticity, but even more pleased when he shared his life's wisdom with the classroom. Since then he has gone on to attend more certifications and always mentors the students in the class by sharing his memories, wit and wisdom from Stone's training sessions.

The biggest takeaway, however, is that David is a doer, not a dreamer. Unfulfilled dreams can be labeled fantasies of the heart, but through action David snatches his dreams out of the ether and makes them go to work for him! This is how he manages to create a heaven on earth for himself, his family, and his staff. Take it from me. Listen to David Gilston's suggestions for taking action, and soon you will find that with this type of follow through you too will have the potential to reach your goals.

Definite Goals Attract Success

Dr. Napoleon Hill

The mind that has been conditioned to receive attracts that which it needs, just as a magnet attracts steel filings. The most difficult part of any task is getting started. Once a start has been made, however, the ways to complete the job become evident.

The truth of this fact has been proved; people with definite goals achieve far greater success than those who have no goals. And I have yet to find a single successful person who did not readily admit that the major turning point in his life came when he adopted a definite major purpose.

No person can tell another what his or her purpose should be, but once you have adopted your own, you will see how the other principles will come into play and inspire you to action.

Your imagination will become more alert and it will reveal to you many opportunities related to your purpose.

Opposition will disappear, and others will give you their friendly cooperation.

Fear and doubt will also disappear, and somewhere along the way you will meet your "other self" face to face— that self which can, and will, carry you to success.

PMA Adviser. December, 1985, Volume 4, Number 12, p. 6.

CHAPTER 38

With our generation's busy schedules and technology all around us it is easy to get lost in it all. Setting time aside to spend with your family is very important for maintaining good communication. Playing table top games together with your family creates a bond of common interest while communicating face to face with each other.

– Jeremy Rayzor

Why not spend time together as a family doing things that can be enjoyed today and also savored tomorrow? It seems that most families spend less time together than before so it is important that the time spent together is enjoyable and educational. Seeking ways to spend time together in active not passive activities can be difficult, but well worth the effort. Perhaps you can create a list of activities that your family would enjoy and next ask members to select a first, second, and third choice of recreational activities to pursue. This will give insight as to the group's interest.

One idea could be to generate interest in doing something that the family can develop a talent in together such as drawing, gardening, woodworking, cooking, craft making, playing musical instruments, care giving for a pet, volunteering for a community or church cause, or reading the same book for group discussion. These choices are all good ways to enhance everyone's skill level. Easily these family activities can contribute to better communication, the enhancement of special talents, familial bonding, and closer personal relationships as everyone participates in and benefits from the selected activity. And, there can be more than one activity. Family members can each select a favorite and turns can be taken in selecting activities that rotate.

Too often we hear of families dealing with problems rather than creating opportunities for enjoyment and recreation. Perhaps by placing more emphasis on doing things that are enjoyable and educational, less emphasis would be placed on dealing with unwanted situations. This may seem simplistic, but it might just work too. It has been said that if we focus on the outcome that we are seeking, we will experience more of that outcome. For example, if you value reading why not create more opportunities to create readers at home? Visit local libraries, bookstores, and showcase slogans such as, "Readers are Leaders," etc. By demonstrating that the art of reading is a special treasure to possess, you will create more opportunities for reading to blossom in your family. Creativity can banish boredom as easily as light eradicates darkness. Isn't it time to let your little light shine for the purpose of creating positive opportunities for your family?

Lead Your Children to Success

Dr. Napoleon Hill

There is a great deal of talk these days about juvenile delinquency and the problems of youth. I'd like to tell the story about one juvenile delinquent and how he was directed into useful pursuits. I was the juvenile delinquent.

My father was a very religious man. There were two of us boys and I was the older, with a mind of my own that defied all of my father's efforts to "reform" me. Our mother had died years before.

I liked firearms and had a couple of pistols hidden in hollow trees on our land in the mountains of southwest Virginia. Because of complaints from the neighbors, my father tracked them down and smashed the weapons with a sledge hammer. I liked mountain music, and had a banjo that I played in secret. But my father's religious learnings were opposed to this, too. He hunted until he found the banjo and destroyed it.

Dancing was forbidden also. But from time to time I managed to "borrow" a horse after Dad was asleep and attend dances in the village.

As a result of all this, my visits to the family woodshed were frequent and terrible. But each appointment in this shrine of horrors only made me more determined to violate the rules whenever I could. I was well on the way to becoming a complete rebel against all of the regulations of society. What saved me was my father's decision to marry again. The stepmother he brought to our mountain cabin was a wonderful, kind and understanding woman.

She bought me a new banjo, and even helped me learn to play it. From a mail order house, she purchased two shiny nickel-plated target pistols—one for herself and the other for me. Then we spent many happy hours together as she taught me to plink at harmless targets instead of at the neighbors' chickens and cows.

Having won my confidence and love by helping me to do the things I wanted to do, she set out to direct my energies to better purposes. She obtained a second hand typewriter and began teaching me how to express ideas on paper. Finally, she helped me get a job as mountain reporter for a "string" of small newspapers. Now I can look back and point to that moment as the most decisive in my life. Is it any wonder that I am grateful to this great lady?

Because of this experience, I'm inclined to take the side of the juvenile delinquents whenever I hear of this problem. Not all delinquency stems from the same causes, of course. But in many cases, I suspect they result from excessively-harsh rules which are too strictly enforced. And I fear, too, that many parents fail to realize that the boundless energy which leads youth into trouble can be easily directed to lead them toward tremendous success. The person who is listless and lazy, lacking the spirit of adventure, is not the one who will achieve great things. Almost all men and women who attain high places in our civilization are "trouble-makers"— free spirits who aren't afraid to defy convention to strike out on new tails, to jar their fellowmen out of their lethargy.

If your child is such a courageous person, be glad. Help him to learn to channel his forceful character toward success in life. Praise him for his willingness to try anything. Show him how to learn from his mistakes when he takes a wrong course.

Above all, give him your praise rather than your condemnation. For somehow it is human nature for people to live up to the reputation which others give them.

Success Unlimited. June, 1965, Vol. 12, No. 6, pp. 33–34.

CHAPTER 39

I heard recently that 25 percent of the world's population makes less than $1 a day and they spend almost all their time just surviving. That certainly makes my life seem pretty extraordinary. We all have much to be thankful for. But compared to where you and I could be if we really applied ourselves in areas of our lives that we would like to improve, is an area certainly worth exploring.

— Vic Conant

Ever wonder how desire begins for one's mission in life? Perhaps it could be as simple as looking over someone's shoulder. Recall as a young adult a person you admired. Perhaps it was a parent, a grandparent, a relative, a teacher, or even someone outside your immediate circle that the world labeled "famous"? Can you specifically recall the traits or characteristics in their personality that you found to be so admirable?

If we ascribe to the idea that values are caught not taught, wouldn't it be good timing to put impressionable children in proximity to people who have something that would be worthwhile catching? Enthusiasm can be very contagious and given the right platform for controlled enthusiasm, people can become inspired and positively motivated to do what they see as valuable themselves. From the Peace Corps to politics to philanthropy, people are motivated to follow in the footsteps of a mission they deem worthy of emulating. And, it is never too early to start to position a young adult on the road to success one principle at a time.

Famous people often leave behind a legacy of books that detail the steps that can be taken to lead a rich and full life. Through reading the classics, individuals can begin to broaden their horizons and discover opportunities for personal advancement. By deciding on a topic of interest, your desire for knowledge in that area can be found in a library and on the Internet. Amazingly, today there is no excuse for lack of information on anything. Information is free for the asking, but the application of acquired information is what makes the difference in our own life.

Drop some hints for the up and coming generation. Leave some books around that are inspirational and value-laden. Occasionally remark how a good book has changed your life. Suggest that it would be wise for others who are dedicated to their personal advancement to read it too. Before long you will have created your own lending library much as Thomas Jefferson and Andrew Carnegie did in the past. And, in doing so, you will continue their legacy in making the world a better place in which to live one good book at a time.

Human Engineering and Enthusiasm

Dr. Napoleon Hill

Hope, enthusiasm, and faith are key words because of their close relationship. When they are combined with definiteness of purpose, they give one access to unlimited mind-power. These are the four factors which lead to a burning desire.

Hope alone is of little value. It is but little more than a wish, and everyone has wishes in abundance. Nothing comes of wishes until they are organized and associated with their companions: definiteness of purpose, enthusiasm, and faith.

Men of great achievement are men of great desires. You will have such desires, and achieve them, if you will follow the instructions you have been given. Remember: Anything in life worth having is worth working for. And there is a price to be paid. The price for reaping the benefits of this philosophy consists mainly in eternal vigilance and everlasting persistence in applying such a philosophy as a daily habit. Mere knowledge is not enough. It must be applied.

PMA Science of Success Course, Educational Edition. Napoleon Hill Foundation, 1961, pp. 262–263.

CHAPTER 40

The point at which time touches eternity is the present. The present moment is the place where we are really free—free of the regrets of the past and also free from the worries about the future. I have likened it to being on vacation or perpetual Christmas because there are gifts in every moment.

– Karen Larsen

What do you think when someone tells you to be present in the moment? Well, I know what I do. I think about what I will fix for dinner, where I will stop on the drive home, and what I will be doing on the weekend! Not exactly what I am supposed to be doing, but because I find it hard to stay in the moment, I either trespass into the future or travel down memory lane.

Living in the past is not a good place to put down roots. Dale Carnegie states, "Don't try to saw sawdust." Good advice. The past is over and what happened in the past should stay there. Lives conforming to past events are stagnant. Nothing new can occur. Replaying old events can stifle a person's day to day experiences. Memories are precious, but living today is more so. Otherwise, you could just become an old rerun.

Living in the future can become an extended daydream too with no foundation or foothold in reality. Always being elsewhere besides where you are can get you into trouble emotionally, socially, physically, financially, mentally, and spiritually. Perhaps it could be a lack of commitment, inability to make a decision, or being afraid of adversity. Whatever propels you into the future might just keep you lost in the imaginary space of your own daydreams unless you decide to plant both your feet on solid ground and get into action now.

Capitalizing upon living in the moment can provide healthy roots so that when wings are needed we can grow those too. Many of you know Don Green, the Executive Director for the Foundation. His mother is now ill. Recently, he was helping her walk across the room with the aid of a walker. As she paused for a moment, he asked her if she knew where she was going. Her response is priceless. Without missing a beat, she stated, "To Heaven." It would surely be a joy to live in each moment of the life we are given, and also to be as certain of our future home as Don's mom is as the time nears.

Peace of Mind and Power of Mind

Dr. Napoleon Hill

Since what you achieve in life depends on what you first conceive, and this depends first of all upon your deep, inner, subconsciously founded belief—you see that your life depends upon your power to believe.

No, your mere life-processes do not depend upon this power. The Eternal has made it possible for the supreme achievement of evolution, man, to stay alive even without knowing he is alive. The beating of the heart, the pumping of the lungs, the processes of digestion and other vital functions are taken care of by a part of the brain which takes care of itself.

Beyond this, man creates an ever better species. He aspires and climbs to the heights of this aspiration. Seeing heights yet beyond, again he aspires—and achieves that peak, beyond which lies another and another.

Significantly, philosophers always have recognized the power of the quiet mind, the peaceful mind. This is far from being a mind empty of aspiration. It is, rather a mind which can hold, judge and evaluate the highest forms of aspiration. Nor is a peaceful mind the exclusive property of a person who does not move about in the world and busy himself with the world's manifold affairs, for some of the most peaceful minds are the busiest. Remember, we speak of inner peace, like a quiet center about which all else revolves, like a great rotating dynamo doing useful work and filled with energy, yet referring its rotation always to the unmoved pivot at its middle.

Grow Rich! WIth Peace of Mind. Fawcett, 1967, pp. 203–204.

CHAPTER 41

You are the only person who can authentically be you. That's what makes you unique. That's your advantage. You know that you are being yourself when you're the same person no matter where you are or who you are with. Be authentic—nobody wants to do business with a phony.

– Brandon Miltsch

Respect is a circle not an arrow. You must give it to receive it. It is reciprocal. And, it doesn't first have to be earned, since everyone is entitled to receive it by nature of being human. Although we may not approve of someone's actions, their manner of dress, their choice of language, their level of education, their work ethic, their financial status, etc., they are still entitled to being treated as equal to and not less than others we may approve of or endorse. Respect is also like a mirror since it allows us to reflect on our own behavior. Unfortunately, many people fail to see that their disrespectful actions only come full circle. As the saying goes, "What goes around comes around...."

Interestingly enough, the person receiving the least of our respect may be our own self. Addictions to work, money, alcohol, drugs, sex, and just about anything else can rob us of essential self-renewal time. To get more of what we already have, we become like a hamster on its toy wheel. I've read that a hamster can travel eight miles per day on its wheel, but never arrive at any destination other than right where it began. Addictions drive us to repetitive behaviors and obscure other aspects of quality life such as family, friends, nature, recreation and the like that are placed on the back burner because our ego believes these "detours" in life may fail to produce more of what will feed our addiction.

Finally, by "disrespecting" others we add characteristics to our personality that may turn others off. By leaning too heavily on "what you can do for me" instead of "what I can do for you" our personal integrity is compromised. Additionally, this attitude doesn't promote teamwork or anything greater. Rather, it promotes resentment and a loss of desire from the person on the receiving end of the demand to perform on call. Ultimately, the person who is disrespected decides to disengage and exit the situation. In the end, the Golden Rule has the best universal message. "Do unto others as you would have others do unto you." Notice it does not say "for you," but "unto you." If the arrow only travels in one direction it is best to make certain in the future that you do not set yourself up to be the target. Think about it. What you get by giving respect is worth more than what you get by demanding it.

Spiritual Food

Dr. Napoleon Hill

Man needs spiritual food just as he needs a properly balanced diet of physical food, and religion is the greatest of all sources from which spiritual food may be obtained.

A man's name on a church membership roll will avail him but little unless he belongs in his own heart and puts something into his religion besides mere passive belief in its soundness, and a dollar in the collection plate now and then. Religion demands doing, not just believing.

True religion gives one humility of heart, sympathy with the unfortunate and a willingness to go the extra mile. It leads to harmony in human relationships, and fosters the principle of the Golden Rule. It strips one of vanity, self-love, excessive ambition, and over-evaluation of material things. It leads inevitably to the attainment of a labor of love, one of the more important of the twelve riches of life.

The man who truly has religion proclaims his religion through his deeds. He lives his religion in his occupation, and it comes back to him greatly multiplied, in his pay envelope, in his peace of mind, and in the harmony he finds with his daily associates.

True religion fosters and develops a positive mental attitude and a willingness to live and let live. It leads to the development of creative vision and inspires self-discipline on a noble scale.

PMA Science of Success Course, Educational Edition. Napoleon Hill Foundation, 1961, pp. 471–472.

CHAPTER 42

You may lose your reputation, your home and even your
family, but you can't lose your capacity to give if you're
learning to give. But you're not really giving if you give to
get something other than a greater capacity to give.

– Charlie "Tremendous" Jones

Today many people are talking about what they get for nothing. From coupons to rebates to gifts with purchase to finders' fees to rewards for information to coins found on the street to extra change from the cashier—and the list goes on and on. With the total emphasis on getting, there is little emphasis on giving. Let's reverse the order and ask ourselves what we give instead of what we get!

Today, did you give a smile to someone without one? Did you lift up a person in the dumps? Did you respond to a phone call, email, letter, or acquaintance with a "yes" instead of a "no?" Did you offer encouragement to someone discouraged? Did you connect someone to another as a favor rather than a bounty hunter performing a service? Did you disregard the "what's in it for me?" pop-up, and give without the expectation of receiving?

Perhaps setting a few goals with the goal in mind to help others would be a good lesson from the giving and not the receiving end. And, one more lesson. Change always begins with you!

Going the Extra Mile Pays

Dr. Napoleon Hill

I chose the principle of Going the Extra Mile for analysis in this column today for the reason that the whole world is rapidly becoming spiritually bankrupt mainly because a majority of the people have put this principle in reverse gear by trying to get something for nothing! I suspect it is because the real spiritual meaning of the rule has not been generally understood. In final analysis it is the Golden Rule streamlined and applied to human relationships in all walks of life. Lloyd Douglas caught the full meaning of this great universal rule and interpreted it in his book, *Magnificent Obsession*, which made a profound impression on those who read the book.

This country may need a two-ocean navy; it may need the largest fleet of airplanes in the world; it may need production of war materials on a huge scale; and I think it needs all these; but what it needs most of all is for the people, all of us, to stop trying to get without giving, and begin now, to Go The Extra Mile, in the same spirit that the 56 men who signed the Declaration of Independence applied this rule, when the "freest and richest" country known to civilization was born.

This is not only the way to salvation of our souls (for some of us seem not so much concerned about our souls as we are about our pocketbooks) but it is the quickest and surest way to self-determination economically, for it is as true as that night follows day, that the man who does more than he is paid for, and does it in a pleasant mental attitude, sooner or later is paid for more than he does. The rule has never been known to fail during the thirty-odd years I have been observing it.

Greenville Piedmont. August 5, 1941.

CHAPTER 43

The entire philosophy of Napoleon Hill is based on the Golden Rule. The Foundation deeply appreciates the support of those of you who only purchase Napoleon Hill authorized books. You can identify these materials by the Foundation logo and by looking inside for the Napoleon Hill copyright.

– Don Green

Ever consider the word plagiarism? It is not a nice word. It means copying someone else's words or thoughts, directly or indirectly via paraphrasing, and stating that these ideas and words are your own. You probably heard about this in school, and as an English teacher I know an easy technique for identifying a plagiarist. All you have to do is ask the person to sit down on the spot and write an essay for you on the same subject without the assistance of any primary or secondary materials. Theory is that if they "authored" what they state they authored, the individual will be able to come up with an essay that has most of the form, tone, and content of the original. And, if they refuse, you can usually assume that they are refusing for a good reason. Reason being, they can't do it because they did not write it.

It's a given fact that we live in a world of "knock-offs." The designer purses, shoes, dresses, watches, etc., that purport to be undistinguishable from the real thing are marketed everywhere. Perhaps, only a fake can be ascertained by one trained in the commodity, however, a fake is just that—not the real thing. Marketers create "knock-offs" for their own benefit in sales. Likewise, people who purport to have the *"real"* Napoleon Hill materials are just using a marketing ploy to get your dollars in their pockets.

I have worked for the Foundation as Director of the Napoleon Hill World Learning Center for over twelve years, and taught for another decade for the Foundation previously. I can assure you that what Don Green has written is accurate regarding the 1937 edition of *Think and Grow Rich*. It is absolutely printed as Napoleon Hill and Rosa Lee Hill released it in 1937.

So, if you want the "real thing" to enjoy, support the Foundation by making your purchase though us. That way, you will continue to honor the legacy of Napoleon Hill and the Foundation that he created. This is the very best way to acknowledge his work.

To Succeed in Life, Succeed in Being Yourself

Dr. Napoleon Hill

You may greatly admire some person for a particular skill or talent he shows. Wishing to exercise a similar skill, you may decide you are going to "be" that person. You will have wasted a great deal of time and effort before you discover that personality is a very subtle thing and that nobody can "be" anyone else without harming his own personality and crippling the drives that can make him great in his own right.

In my youth I decided to write the way Arthur Brisbane wrote. He was a very versatile and capable writer with a huge following, and I thought I was being smart when I set out to copy his style. A friend brought me up short when he remarked that if I copied Brisbane I would never develop a style of my own. Right then I put Brisbane aside, and the success of my writings has justified my decision not be to Arthur Brisbane but to be Napoleon Hill.

Children try to imitate older people, which is understandable. I see many a grown-up child trying to keep up with the Joneses financially, or trying to keep up the social pace that the Smiths set, with disastrous results. Until you are willing to be your own self, at your own level, you cannot know yourself, nor know what your mind can accomplish.

Grow Rich! With Peace of Mind. Ballantine, 1996, p. 118.

CHAPTER 44

The good news is that human beings are capable of achieving almost anything they put their minds to. The problem does not lie in inability, but rather in lack of clarity. Most people have not been able to identify their life goal, and if there is no goal, there is no plan.

– Phil Taylor

Ralph Waldo Emerson states, "Unless you try to do something beyond what you have already mastered, you will never grow."

Instinctively we know this, but sometimes it feels better and more natural to rest on our laurels. The real message that needs to be told is that aspiring to learn something new, learning it, and then applying it, involve hard work and commitment. But, when the learning is accomplished and integrated into who we are, we have a sense of fulfillment that far exceeds the familiar smug feeling of thinking that we are more than we are.

Praise comes easily for a child taking his first steps, for a poem memorized and recited, for a dance routine flawlessly performed, for a public piano recital, or for the earned diploma. The recognition of these "firsts" is due to the newness of the accomplishment, and not generally for repeated performances that become mundane.

"Firsts" have a huge emotional payoff for the individual. In order to keep that deposit coming into our Bank of Self-Esteem account, we need to challenge ourselves to out-perform our current abilities. Whether the challenge is in physical endurance, mental enhancement, or spiritual formation, we need to strive to be our very best. Nothing else is worth the effort.

When we give it our very best and succeed, our "can-do" level is raised, and so is our self-esteem. Maybe we won't walk on the moon, but we might walk through the doors of a university and register for a class. Or, we might walk up to the front desk and ask for a job application. Better yet, we might just stay engaged and continue to walk the talk that leads to ultimate success each day of our lives. Why not? Isn't it a worthy choice?

Get Ready to Succeed

Dr. Napoleon Hill & W. Clement Stone

Think of it! Think of the people who drift aimlessly thru life, dissatisfied, struggling against a great many things, but without a clear-cut goal. Can you state, right now, what it is that you want out of life? Fixing your goals may not be easy. It may even involve some painful self-examination. But it will be worth whatever effort it costs, because as soon as you can name your goal, you can expect to enjoy many advantages. These advantages come almost automatically.

1. The first great advantage is that your subconscious mind begins to work under a universal law: "What the mind can conceive and believe—the mind can achieve." Because you visualize your intended destination, your subconscious mind is affected by this self-suggestion. It goes to work to help you get there.

2. Because you know what you want, there is a tendency for you to try to get on the right track and head in the right direction. You get into action.

3. Work now becomes fun. You are motivated to pay the price. You budget your time and money. You study, think, and plan. The more you think about your goals, the more enthusiastic you become. And with enthusiasm your desire turns into a burning desire.

4. You become alerted to opportunities that will help you achieve your objectives as they present themselves in your everyday experiences. Because you know what you want, you are more likely to recognize these opportunities.

When you have a Positive Mental Attitude, the problems of your world tend to bow before you. The payoff is success, health, happiness, wealth.

Chicago Sunday Tribune Magazine. June 19, 1960, pp. 37–39.

CHAPTER 45

What do we need to change? The answer is, everything we need to in order to make what we want a reality. Sometimes we need to change our thoughts, feelings or actions. We can't get what we want by being the person we are right now. If that were the case, we would already have the thing. So something must change inside of us.

– Michael Joesten

Change is a process that most people do not like to undertake. Whether it's a change in jobs, homes, relationships, memberships, etc., in almost all areas people complain about the change process. Instead of embracing the new that is approaching on the horizon, people lament the old that is slipping away. You might think of it as the dawn and the sunset. Both occurrences are beautiful and serve to enhance each other. Yet alone, a lifetime of sunsets would not be the same as a lifetime that experiences both.

Looking at change from a different perspective, it would be a happier and easier process if we looked at what we are gaining rather than what we are losing. Think of it as the yin and the yang of the universe. Without change we would become stagnant. Stagnant water stinks. It is not drinkable, and no one wants to swim in it. Animals avoid it and people do too.

Conversely, living water is water that flows and refreshes itself and its boundaries. It invites us to its shores as we watch and listen to the process. It invigorates us rather than depresses us. Change can be that way too if we allow ourselves to see it from the angle of newness.

Being part of the here and now requires us to embrace change. A change in routine, diet, exercise, or in whatever else has become stagnant in our lives, can change our world. It does not have to be monumental to make a difference in our lives, but we do have to begin the process. It could be as simple as a thirty minute walk during the day that can be the start of further change.

Why not challenge yourself to the change process if you feel you are stuck in a stagnant life? Find a small change to make that is non-threatening at first, and then do it. Like the snowball that gathers speed and size as it rolls downhill, I just bet you will find that everything about change is not negative. And, there is much more of the positive that you will like to explore in this process when you take that first bold step toward gifting yourself with more of life!

Something for Nothing

Dr. Napoleon Hill

No one can get something for nothing. Everything worth having has a definite price, and that price must be paid. The rules of personal achievement are as definite as the rules of mathematics. If ever there was a true science, it is the science of personal achievement described in the seventeen principles of this philosophy.

You are a student of this philosophy. Therefore you are deprived of alibis for failure, including the grandfather of them all, "I never had an opportunity." You have an opportunity, and it lies in the privilege of availing yourself of the combined knowledge of more than five hundred men of great achievement who have made this philosophy available to you.

What are you going to do with your opportunity?

Success does not require a great amount of knowledge about anything, but it does call for the persistent use of whatever knowledge you may have.

How are you using your time?

How much of it are you wasting, and how are you wasting it?

What are you going to do to stop this waste?

PMA Science of Success Course, Educational Edition. Napoleon Hill Foundation, 1961, pp. 460–461.

CHAPTER 46

Turning adversity into unlimited opportunity is about removing the roadblocks that we set up for ourselves. As you remove these roadblocks, a sacred peace that was always there shines forth. I was able to take my childhood adversity and turn it around 360 degrees into a positive course of action for growth, valuable learning, and purpose.

— Taylor Tagg

Respect is not a four-letter word, but a seven-letter word. Like Shakespeare's Seven Stages of Life, the Seven Sacraments, the Seven Chakras, and other multiples that come in sevens, respect is something that is gained and given in stages or in the process, and is not inherited or innate at birth. Respect is acquired in stages, and can also be lost in a moment. Don't take the risk and lose what you have gained by a slovenly approach in dealing with others.

When you treat people with respect, they in turn begin to respect you and tend to treat you in a reciprocal fashion. When you disrespect someone, animosity can be the result. Disrespect does not only apply to words or language, but also to such things as manners, courtesy, dress, and personal habits.

For example, if you dine in a nice restaurant but leave the table a mess, taunt the waitress, or demand service your superior attitude will gain you no respect. The joy will be witnessed in your leaving and not in the fact that you graced the establishment with your presence. You will have to decide for yourself what effect you want to leave on people you interact with in life. If you want to be remembered as an uncouth and insensitive person, fail to be respectful and you will achieve your goal.

The legacy of respect that you leave behind will be in your parting not in your presence.

Remember in grade school, you learned the words "Please" and "Thank You?" Also, you learned that pointing at a person with your index finger in a demanding fashion left three fingers pointing back at yourself—the real culprit. Your mother probably told you to respect your elders, clean your room, listen more than you speak, as well as a long litany of other sage pieces of advice.

It is not too late to refashion your life and your manners. Hold the door for someone, express your gratitude, clean up after yourself, refuse to demand service but request it. It is likely that you will be more successful in achieving what you want in both the short and long term if you remember your manners! The trait of Pleasing Personality begins and ends with you. Otherwise, you just might have to experience a little Adversity and Defeat prior to learning the other lesson!

A Recommended Formula for Getting Rid of Guilt

Dr. Napoleon Hill

First of all, you listen as you hear advice, a lecture, an inspirational sermon that could change your life.

... Then you count your blessings, and thank God for them. Feel sincerely sorry and ask for forgiveness. When you realize your blessings, it isn't difficult to become sincerely sorry for the wrongs you have done. And truly to repent. Then you will have the courage to ask for forgiveness from God.

... You must take the first step forward. This is important because it is a symbol through a physical gesture that you make in the direction of a changed life. When Jim walked down the aisle, he was making a public announcement that he had become sorry for his past and was now ready to change his life.

... Also, you must make amends by taking the second step forward: begin immediately to right every wrong.

... And then the most important step of all: apply the Golden Rule. This should be easy. For now when you are tempted to do wrong, that "still, small voice" will whisper to you. And when it does, stop and listen. Count your blessings. Picture yourself in the other fellow's place. And then make your decision to do what you would want done if you actually were in his position.

Success Through a Positive Mental Attitude. Prentice-Hall, 1960, p. 210.

CHAPTER 47

With the proliferation of products, services, and information around the globe, many breakthrough inventions today come from new applications for existing products or services. These kinds of cutting-edge, breakthrough developments don't come from having all the answers. They come from constantly asking questions.

— Jim Stovall

We are all capable of using the principle of creative vision. Napoleon Hill teaches us that there are two types of imagination: synthetic imagination and creative imagination. Although synthetic imagination is the more common of the two, it is equally valuable because it builds on something that previously existed while putting that "something" to a new use. If you ever read newspaper columns that suggest innovative uses for existing products such as coffee cans, old newspapers, vinegar, paper tubes, and on and on, you get the idea. Ecologically speaking it is good to use products up rather than throwing them out!

Synthetic imagination challenges us to arrange existing thoughts, ideas, plans, items, or facts into a new order for a new outcome. A fun classroom activity is to give a team a product that they cannot readily identify and ask them what it is used for in the home or business. It can be a hilarious activity to list the uses the group comes up with before they learn the intended purpose of the product. It's also a good routine for sparking synthetic imagination.

Creative imagination is best described as a spark of genius that comes to us through our sixth sense. It could be viewed as a "download" from Infinite Intelligence. This "knowing" enables a new form of creation to enter into the world. It might have been captured by the first person who decided to use fire for cooking and warmth and also the first person who foresaw that lightning that was harnessed could bring the gift of electricity to the world.

Dreams define us because by dreaming we can anticipate an even better world for ourselves and for humanity. When we visualize something and bring it down to earth we begin the process of creation in its ultimate sense. Something from nothing is the end result of dreaming. It allows us to transfer the ethereal into the material and thereby bring the gift to the world in a usable, concrete form.

Rainbows, stardust, thunder, lightning, wind, smells, and other sensory phenomena can gift us with a desire to utilize a pure essence in the here and now. By capturing the spirit in the acorn, in time an enormous oak tree is delivered that offers beauty and shelter to its surroundings. The essence of lightning is transmuted energy that results in electricity. A cleaner and a safer method of providing light and heat for our homes.

What do you see that exists outside of the normal world? Perhaps it is what dreams are made of, and by recalling these dreams and releasing their blessings we can indeed improve the world we live in one small step at a time.

Awaken the Sleeping Giant Within You

Dr. Napoleon Hill

For you are a mind with a body. And your mind consists of dual, invisible gigantic powers: the conscious and the subconscious. One is a giant that never sleeps. It is called the subconscious mind. The other is a giant which when asleep is powerless. When awakened, his potential power is unlimited. This giant is known as the conscious mind. When the two work in harmony, they can affect, use, control or harmonize with all known and unknown powers.

What wouldst thou have? "What wouldst thou have? I am ready to obey thee as thy slave —I and the other slaves of the lamp," said the genie.

Awaken the sleeping giant within you! It is more powerful than all the genii of Aladdin's lamp! The genii are fictional. Your sleeping giant is real!

What wouldst thou have? Love? Good health? Success? Friends? Money? A home? A car? Recognition? Peace of mind? Courage? Happiness? Or, would you make your world a better world in which to live? The sleeping giant within you has the power to bring your wishes into reality. What wouldst thou have? Name it and it's yours.

Awaken the sleeping giant within you! How?

Think. Think with a positive mental attitude.

Success Through a Positive Mental Attitude. Prentice-Hall, 1960, pp.234–235.

CHAPTER 48

Why are stories powerful? Because the deepest truth is often found through stories. One of the missing elements in today's society is that we have lost sight of the value of a story. In most ancient cultures, the wisdom and understanding of the human condition were explored and passed down that way.

— Karen Larsen

With the year-end holidays upon us, it is only natural to recall events from past celebrations that resonate with us for a lifetime. As we reflect on times past, it often is not the most expensive gift, or the decorations of the season that stay with us. Rather it is the caring and thoughtfulness of family and friends who graced our holiday celebrations that we most recall. Think for a moment about your best personal memories. Do they bring a smile to your face even now? Do they warm your heart in the afterglow of the moment? Are they worth sharing? Why not begin to write these memories down as a gift to future generations yet unborn? Otherwise, with your passing these precious memories will be lost forever.

I like to believe that memories we cherish serve more than just giving us happy thoughts that fulfill no other purpose.

Rather, the story of our life reminds us that each of us is unique, put here for a purpose. We can't be replaced since each and every one of us is an original. No other person can accomplish the task we were put here to do. Therefore, our experiences, background, culture, memories, and life's work are all significant. I bet that there are questions that you would like to ask departed relatives, friends, and acquaintances that you did not bother with when they were living. But, those questions cannot be asked now.

As you create your holiday correspondence, think on these things and write now in time to be ready for the holidays. Below are some questions to get you started. Answer the ones that bring back memories you cherish, and tuck your responses inside your family's Holiday Greetings. I bet this year's card won't be thrown out with the gift wrappings if you sincerely share from the heart!

1. What is my favorite holiday memory growing up?

2. What song or carol ushers in the season for me?

3. What tradition do I cherish and practice each year?

4. Recalling a parent or relative, who made the holiday for me as a youngster and how did they do it?

5. Emotionally, the holiday season fills me with gratitude when…? Happy Sharing!

The American Yuletide Spirit

Dr. Napoleon Hill

As one year ends and another begins, and while the Yuletide spirit is yet alive, let us stop for a moment and consider some of the blessings for which we should be thankful. Let us take a personal inventory of our Divine rewards and see whether or not the year, which has moved us a step closer to the great unknown beyond, has helped make us a truly better and further advanced civilization.

I have no right or desire to judge the degree of advancement which others have made, or what blessings they have received, but personally I have much for which I am truly thankful.

FIRST, I have been abundantly blessed with good health and strength of both body and mind.

SECOND, I have two fine young boys and their darling mother who are also blessed with health and strength of body and mind. These dear ones are a constant source of inspiration to me in my efforts to be a successful businessman and a loyal and patriotic American.

THIRD, I possess the undisturbed right to labor freely for these loved ones in my selected vocation in a country that offers an abundance of encouragement and protection to the legitimate producer of human necessities.

FOURTH, I enjoy citizenship in a country that is free from war and its attendant suffering, a country where love for peace, respect for the home, and reverence of God are dominant in the minds of its people.

FIFTH, I enjoy the commercial monument which I have steadily built up with the help of many others and through my own long hours of effort and unceasing determination. I shall not pass into the New Year without seeing my dreams of success realized.

SIXTH, I have no fault to find with anyone on earth. I am at peace with all my fellowmen. I am in a state of mental attitude which leave me free to work effectively and aggressively during the New Year. If I have done any good deeds during the past year, I hope to double them during the next. If I have been useful to any human being during the old year, I hope to be doubly useful during the New Year.

This was adapted from a message written by Napoleon Hill at the beginning of 1915 when he was president of the Betsy Ross Candy Shop System in Chicago, more than two decades before he published his classic best-seller, *Think and Grow Rich*.

CHAPTER 49

What did you love to do as a kid? If you reflect, you can find things to bring back to light the ease and fun you then had. Did you know that there is something that you do better than most? Have you ever thought of a business, a way of wanting to help others, or ideas for making money, that you never acted on?

– Greg Etherton

Doing what we enjoy doing makes life less tedious. Think back to when you anticipated something fully and enjoyed the planning process as much as the actual event. When planning for something we enjoy doing, the day to day activities take on new hope coupled with the promise of a brighter future. Perhaps this is the effect of the force field surrounding a positive mental attitude. By lifting our mood from the tedium of the day to day, we not only peak our interest in the moment but anticipate our future in a positive light. And, we all know that what we think about we bring about!

I often reflect on Norman Cousins' book, *The Anatomy of an Illness,* and how he treated himself with daily doses of humor. By tuning in to what makes us laugh it has been said that we are giving ourselves a massage from the inside out! And, in the process, we can assist in our own healing. This is one application of maintaining a positive mental attitude that really works in our physical well-being.

By watching comedies, humorous sitcoms, and listening to the funny acts of old radio personalities, we can lift our spirits through laughter. Humor removes weariness, it sharpens our senses, it lightens our load, and it clears our minds. Just by laughing out loud, we are demonstrating to the world that we are cultivating a positive mental attitude.

It seems that adults laugh less and less. Laughter is becoming a lost art. People do not laugh out loud, but rather complain out loud. Sincere, not raucous, laughter possesses an infection that is contagious. People catch the laughter and allow it to overtake them as if they were catching something physical. Laughter awakens us to the brighter side of existence and reminds us that all need not be dreary and forlorn once we meet midlife.

Take the challenge of cultivating laughter daily. Watch something that makes you laugh and get accustomed to the feeling. Let your response grow by feeding and watering it daily. Like a new seed, it is just waiting to sprout with your care and encouragement. Perhaps the fruit of this laughter will be the tastiest treat that you have given yourself in a long time. Go ahead! Smile. Grin. Laugh. Laugh out loud! You will feel the better for it.

Enjoy Good Health and Live Longer

Dr. Napoleon Hill & W. Clement Stone

Positive Mental Attitude plays an important role in your health and your day-to-day energies and enthusiasms for your life and your work. "Every day in every way, through the grace of God, I am getting better and better," is no pie-in-the-sky jargon for the man who recites the sentence several times each day upon awakening and again before going to bed.

In one sense, he is putting PMA forces to work for him. He is using the forces which attract the better things of life to him. He is using the forces which the authors of *Success Through a Positive Mental Attitude* want you to use.

How PMA aids you: PMA will help you develop mental and physical health and a longer life. And NMA will just as surely undermine mental and physical health and shorten your life. It all depends upon which side of the talisman you turn up. Positive Mental Attitude properly employed has saved the lives of many persons because someone close to them had a strong Positive Mental Attitude.

It has been written: "So we do not lose heart.... Because we look not to the things that are seen but to the things that are unseen; for the things that are seen are transient, but the things that are unseen are eternal."

Success Through a Positive Mental Attitude. Prentice-Hall, 1960, pp. 189–190.

CHAPTER 50

The simple act of walking the labyrinth pattern can be a symbolic act of your persistent action towards your main objective. In the labyrinth you become aware of the intuitive pulses coming from Infinite Intelligence.

— *Uriel Martinez*

Persistence is the key to making your visions a reality. By staying focused on what inspires and thrills you in life, you bring about the truly wonderful aspects of your unique presence into the moment. Just by "doing" you create your own reality in what you want to bring about. When you concentrate on something that potentially fulfills your heart's desire, you bring that reality closer to your present day world.

Remember as children how the Sears and Montgomery Wards catalogs came to our homes in the nick of time for Christmas shopping? Do you remember studying the pages and dreaming about certain items as if they were already in your possession? Next, can you remember when your parents told you to circle what it is that you really, really hoped Santa would bring to you? This first step in the envisioning process is crucial because we "see" with our mind's eye how our dreams could become reality. If our wishes weren't too expensive probably one or two of the items we longed for appeared under the tree on Christmas Eve. Our parents' gift was received in the giving, and our gift was our heart's desire in that young, tender moment. Just watch the holiday classic *A Christmas Story* to see how this plays out. Ralphie is each and every one of us, and that is exactly why the movie has universal appeal. I still have my Red Ryder BB gun!

As we grew up and learned about the process for receiving things, we went to school, held jobs, and practiced the saving process in order to achieve that first car, that better outfit, or even that high school trip overseas. Persistence paid off because we stayed the course and held our longing in our mind's eye until it materialized right in front of us.

By staying prepared, alert, and persistent, we can accomplish many tasks. Now, when I am overwhelmed with many things to do at once, I simply ask my "Higher Self" what is the very next thing I should do to complete the task at hand. Always, an answer surfaces and if I follow my own higher directive I can get much more accomplished than it I worried over a much too long To-Do list. These intuitive nudges work for me, and once I clear away the cobwebs in my thinking, the best plan of attack surfaces and brings me the results that I want. Don't argue with yourself when a plan surfaces. Just follow through, and you will have arrived at your heart's true desire with time to spare.

Imagination

Dr. Napoleon Hill

This lesson on imagination might be called the "hub" of this Reading Course, because every lesson of the course leads to this lesson and makes use of the principle upon which it is based, just as all the telephone wires lead to the exchange office for their source of power. You will never have a definite purpose in life, you will never have self-confidence, you will never have initiative and leadership unless you first create these qualities in your imagination and see yourself in possession of them.

Just as the oak tree develops from the germ that lies in the acorn, and the bird develops from the germ that lies asleep in the egg, so will your material achievements grow out of the organized plans that you create in your imagination. First comes the thought; then organization of that thought into ideas and plans; then transformation of those plans into reality. The beginning, as you will observe, is in your imagination.

The imagination is both interpretative and creative in nature. It can examine facts, concepts and ideas, and it can create new combinations and plans out of these.

Through its interpretative capacity the imagination has one power not generally attributed to it, namely, the power to register vibrations and thought waves that are put into motion from outside sources, just as the radio-receiving apparatus picks up the vibrations of sound. The principle through which this interpretative capacity of the imagination functions is called telepathy; the communication of thought from one mind to another, at long or short distances, without the aid of physical or mechanical appliances, in the manner explained in the Introductory Lesson of this course.

Law of Success. Napoleon Hill Foundation, 1999, Lesson 6, p. 6.

CHAPTER 51

It's easy to stay off the naughty list if you remember this: there is no greater gift than to share your time with another person, to share wholeheartedly without expectation of return.

– Santa

This holiday season let's focus on raising everyone's positive mental attitude awareness. Gifts of the spirit are free of cost and easy to deliver. A smile, a word of praise, recognition, companionship, time spent in doing daily activities such as washing the dishes, caring for pets, attending services, and joining in a Christmas carol played on the radio are all things we can do spontaneously that raise our PMA bar.

Whether it's visiting Santa at the local mall, sledding with small children, taking a nature walk, admiring seasonal decorations, making special treats, or cooking the traditional turkey or ham, the spirit that we bring to the season is what creates the memories of a lifetime.

Although depression is a problem that exists for many until the new year, we can work to alleviate this sour mood by suggesting activities that involve the spiritual, physical, social and mental aspects of the person rather than the financial or emotional aspects which tend to bring about past feelings of regret. By focusing on how we can lifts others' spirits now rather than gift them with material items, we may truly be giving them the best gift of the season.

Right now, why not commit to eradicating negative mental attitudes from your environment? These are attitudes that evolve from complaining, gossiping, comparing, hoarding, witholding, and failing to communicate with others. Doing these actions never raises our spirits and instead causes us to cycle downward until the cloud of depression envelops us and sucks the joy out of the season.

Don't give in; rather launch the PMA Goodwill Counter-Attack. For every NMA thought or action, immediately create a PMA thought or action to remedy the situation. Like an elixir of goodwill, our drink should be the milk of human kindness, as the Spirit of Christmas Yet to Come reminds Scrooge in *A Christmas Carol.* The remedy is simple. The key is putting it to use. Raise your glass filled with PMA and toast the season! Blessings to you and yours now and for all the years ahead!

Contentment

Dr. Napoleon Hill

The richest man in all the world lives in Happy Valley. He is rich in values that endure, in things he cannot lose—things that provide him with contentment, sound health, peace of mind and harmony within his soul.

Here is an inventory of his riches and how he acquired them:

"I found happiness by helping others to find it.

"I found sound health by living temperately and eating only the food my body requires to maintain itself.

"I hate no man, envy no man, but love and respect all mankind.

"I am engaged in a labor of love with which I mix play generously; therefore, I seldom grow tired.

"I pray daily, not for more riches but for more wisdom with which to recognize, embrace, and enjoy the great abundance of riches I already possess.

"I speak no name save only to honor it, and I slander no man for any cause whatsoever.

"I ask no favors of anyone except the privilege of sharing my blessings with all who desire them.

"I am on good terms with my conscience; therefore, it guides me accurately in everything I do.

"I have more material wealth than I need because I am free from greed and covet only those things I can use constructively while I live. My wealth comes from those whom I have benefited by sharing my blessings.

"The estate of Happy Valley which I own is not taxable. It exists mainly in my own mind, in intangible riches that cannot be assessed for taxation or appropriated except by those who adopt my way of life. I created this estate over a lifetime of effort by observing nature's laws and forming habits to conform with them."

Success Through a Positive Mental Attitude. Prentice-Hall, 1960, pp. 211–212.

CHAPTER 52

As I am writing this, I am sitting in my home office, surrounded by books and pictures that cause me to think about how you, and others, think and feel. I was feeling and thinking somewhat negatively. Increased pain and achiness and fatigue disrupted my positive thinking briefly. Then I looked around at the walls and my attitude soon shifted dramatically.

— Tom Cunningham

Do you have a special place at home where you go just to "be?" It can be a special room or a little space that is off in a corner that holds objects, photos, a small collection, and all things "dear" that bring you peace and a feeling of "all's right with the world" when you rest in their presence. As I look around my home, I find many things that remind me of the people they represent and the animals I love. They also present a projection of myself and my interests. Books of many genres, CDs, pictures that remind me of places I have been, and photos of family and friends are in each room of my home. All these things combined express the good times I've enjoyed and when I see them at a glance, they can and do lift my spirit.

My special area of interest is writing. So, my journals hold my memories too. When I jot something down I remember it longer. It sticks with me and announces its importance in my day-to-day routine. A birthday, an item on a to-do list, a recipe, an idea brewing in my head, all take on extra importance when I write it down. I have noticed at special sites worldwide that there are places to write down petitions. Whether it is a request, a prayer, a thanksgiving, or just an observation, by writing it down and leaving it in full view for anyone to read, the Universe is put on notice.

Napoleon Hill says that it is important to brainstorm our ideas and to write them down. Just leaving ideas to float around in the "ether" does not bring them down to our level of existence. Before anything at all happens, it is at first a thought. Next, we capture that thought with our "thought" net, and finally we drag this thought into our here and now. That's when it begins to live up to its potential. Thoughts captured or rescued from the imagination now can be birthed and given real life. What thoughts do you have waiting to be born? Maybe they are waiting for you in your special place of meditation. If you call it an office, a meditation corner, or even a thought palace, it doesn't matter.

The purpose is to locate your desires, bring them into sharper focus, and make them real as you present the gift of yourself to the world.

I wonder what gifts are waiting for you to unwrap?

Little Circumstances

Dr. Napoleon Hill

Success in life is made up of many little circumstances which most people never recognize as being of value to themselves. Failure likewise is made up of small circumstances which go unnoticed by those who fail. A great industrialist once said: Friction in machinery is costly, but friction in the relationships of men who operate machinery is fatal—both to themselves and their associate workers.

Team work in a spirit of friendliness costs so little in the way of time and effort, and it pays such huge dividends, not only in money but in the finer things of life. One wonders why so many people go out of their way to make life miserable for themselves and others by failure to recognize this truth. A kindly word here, a kindly deed there, a pleasant smile everywhere, and this world would be a better place for all mankind.

This is the spirit which lights the path to Happy Valley for all who adopt it. And it is the spirit which leads to the attainment of the twelve riches of life: a positive mental attitude, sound physical health, harmony in human relationships, freedom from fear, the hope of achievement, the capacity for faith, a willingness to share one's blessings, a labor of love, an open mind on all subjects, self-discipline, the capacity to understand people, and last but not least, economic security. What an array of riches, and each of them tied in with that little phrase "team work!"

PMA Science of Success Course, Educational Edition. Napoleon Hill Foundation, 1961, pp. 361–362.

*"Whatever the mind can conceive and believe,
the mind can achieve."*

Napoleon Hill

For more information about Napoleon Hill and available products, please contact the following locations:

Napoleon Hill World Learning Center
Purdue University Calumet
2300 173rd Street
Hammond, Indiana 46323-2094

Judith Williamson, Director
Uriel "Chino" Martinez, Assistant & Graphic Designer

Telephone: 219.989.3173 or 219.989.3166
Email: nhf@purduecal.edu

The Napoleon Hill Foundation
University of Virginia–Wise
College Relations Apt. C
1 College Avenue
Wise, Virginia 24293

Don Green, Executive Director
Annedia Sturgill, Executive Assistant

Telephone: 276.328.6700
Email: napoleonhill@uvawise.edu
Website: www.naphill.org